Australia

by Anne Matthews

English-born Anne Matthews emigrated to Sydney in 1979 and has long been an Australian citizen. As a freelance travel writer specialising in Australian topics, she has travelled widely and written or contributed to numerous travel volumes and guidebooks, including the AA's *Essential Sydney, CityPack Sydney, Thomas Cook Travellers Sydney & New South Wales, Explorer Australia, Tour Guide Australia, Great Highways of the World* and several Fodor *Australia* guidebooks.

Above: *Sydney Harbour and the Opera House*

AA Publishing

A lifeguard on famous Bondi Beach

Find out more about AA Publishing and the wide range of travel publications and services the AA provides by visiting our website at www.theAA.com/travel

Written by Anne Matthews

First published 1998. Reprinted Jun 1998
Revised edition 2000. Reprinted May 2001
Reprinted Apr 2002. Information verified and updated.
Reprinted Oct 2002. Reprinted 2004 with amendments
Reprinted 2005. Information verified and updated.
Reprinted May and Aug 2005
Reprinted Jan and Aug 2006

Published by AA Publishing, a trading name of Automobile Association Developments Limited, whose registered office is Fanum House, Basing View, Basingstoke, Hampshire, RG21 4EA. Registered number 1878835.

A CIP catalogue record for this book is available from the British Library.

A03178

Colour separation: BTB Digital Imaging Limited, Whitchurch, Hampshire
Printed and bound in Italy by Printer Trento S.r.l.

Contents

About this Book 4

Viewing Australia 5–14

Anne Matthews' Australia	6
Australia's Features	7
Essence of Australia	8–9
The Shaping of Australia	10–11
Natural Australia	12–13
Australia's Famous	14

Top Ten 15–26

Cairns and District	16
The Gold Coast	17
The Great Barrier Reef	18–19
Great Ocean Road	20
Kakadu National Park	21
The Kimberley	22
Blue Mountains	23
Sydney Harbour and Sydney Opera House	24
Tasmania's World Heritage Area	25
Uluṟu-Kata Tjuṯa National Park	26

What To See 27–90

New South Wales	30–43
Food and Drink	44–5
Queensland	46–55
Victoria and Tasmania	56–67
In the Know	68–9
South Australia and Northern Territory	70–81
Western Australia	82–90

Where To... 91–116

Eat and Drink	92–9
Stay	100–3
Shop	104–9
Take Children	110–11
Be Entertained	112–16

Practical Matters 117–24

Index 125–6

Acknowledgments 126

About this Book

KEY TO SYMBOLS

Throughout the guide a few straightforward symbols are used to denote the following categories:

- map reference to the maps in the What to See section
- address
- telephone number
- opening times
- restaurant or café on premises or nearby
- nearest subway station
- nearest bus/tram route
- nearest overground train station
- nearest ferry stop
- facilities for visitors with disabilities
- admission charge
- other places of interest nearby
- other practical information
- ➤ indicates the page where you will find a fuller description

This book is divided into five sections to cover the most important aspects of your visit to Australia.

Viewing Australia pages 5–14
An introduction to Australia by the author.
Australia's Features
Essence of Australia
The Shaping of Australia
Peace and Quiet
Australia's Famous

Top Ten pages 15–26
The author's choice of the Top Ten places to visit in Australia, each with practical information.

What to See pages 27–90
The five main areas of Australia, each with its own brief introduction and an alphabetical listing of the main attractions.
Practical information
Snippets of 'Did You Know...' information
3 suggested walks
4 suggested tours
2 features

Where To... pages 91–116
The best places to eat, stay, shop, take children and be entertained.

Practical Matters pages 117–24
A highly visual section containing essential travel information.

Maps
All map references are to the individual maps found in the What to See section of this guide.
For example, Sydney Harbour Bridge has the reference 32B5 – indicating the page on which the map is located and the grid square in which the bridge can be found.
A list of the maps that have been used in this travel guide can be found in the index.

Prices
Where appropriate, an indication of the cost of an establishment is given by **£** signs:
£££ denotes higher prices, **££** denotes average prices, while **£** denotes lower charges.

Star Ratings
Most of the places described in this book have been given a separate rating:

✪✪✪	Do not miss
✪✪	Highly recommended
✪	Worth seeing

Viewing Australia

Anne Matthews' Australia 6
Australia's Features 7
Essence of Australia 8–9
The Shaping of Australia 10–11
Natural Australia 12–13
Australia's Famous 14

Above: *a young surfer*
Right: *a cuddly koala*

Anne Matthews' Australia

Discovery and Settlement

For centuries man believed in the existence of some great southern landmass, but it was not until the 17th century that European seafarers sighted Australia's western coast. Then, in 1770, James Cook discovered the continent's east coast, and eighteen years later the first reluctant 'settlers' – British convicts and soldiers – arrived to disrupt the isolated existence of the Aboriginal people who had lived here for over 50,000 years.

From its unpromising convict beginnings, Australia has developed into a wealthy and politically stable nation of over 20 million people. Since the early days of dependence on Britain, the national self-esteem has grown decade by decade for the past 200 or so years, and Australia successfully showcased its confidence and vibrancy to the world at the Sydney 2000 Olympic Games.

Although proud of its pioneering history and Outback traditions, this is the world's most urbanised society, with 88 per cent of the population living in towns and cities. Most of these settlements are around the coast – far away from the vast and inhospitable interior that takes up a large percentage of the continent's area.

Australia – variously known as 'Down Under', 'Oz', and the 'best address on earth' – is vast: approximately 24 times the size of the British Isles and as big as continental USA (without Alaska). The terrain and climate obviously vary considerably, but overall the weather is warm and sunny, and the scenery varies from interesting to magnificent.

This benign climate has undoubtedly affected the Australian character, best described as egalitarian and relaxed. Aussies are friendly and laid-back, and visitors from everywhere are welcomed enthusiastically. This is a successfully multicultural nation where, despite some intolerance towards Aborigines in particular, people of European, Asian, Arabic, Pacific Island and other origins live together in relative harmony.

Visitors should remember that Australia is enormous – it is over 4,000km from Sydney to Perth – so unless you have months to spare, select your destinations carefully.

Many ancient Aboriginal rock art sites are scattered throughout the continent

Sydney's famous Opera House, completed in 1973, is an unmistakable symbol of Australia's largest city

Australia's Features

Natural Features

- Australia is the world's smallest and flattest continent and, after Antarctica, the driest.
- Australia's coastline is an incredible 36,700km.
- Australia's highest point is Mount Kosciuszko in southern New South Wales – a mere 2,228m high. The lowest point is 16m below sea level at Lake Eyre in Outback South Australia.
- The Great Barrier Reef is the world's largest living, growing structure – it is composed primarily of coral polyps and algae, and stretches for over 2,000km along the Queensland coast.

The modern architecture of Darling Harbour frames some of Sydney's tallest buildings

Make-up and People

- Australia is made of six states – New South Wales, Queensland, Victoria, Tasmania, South Australia and Western Australia; two territories – the Australian Capital Territory (the location of Canberra, the national capital) and the Northern Territory; and external territories, including Norfolk Island and Christmas Island.
- Although of a similar size to the United States (population over 250 million), and 24 times the size of Britain, Australia is home to only 20 million people. Just over 4 million live in Sydney, the largest city.
- In 2001 the number of overseas-born Australians was 4.5 million (23 per cent of the population), and 25 per cent of those born here had at least one overseas-born parent.

Road and Rail

- Australia has more than 810,000km of roads, but only 35 per cent are sealed with bitumen or concrete.
- The world's longest straight stretch of railway is in Outback Western Australia – it is 478.4km long.

Odds and Ends

- Although shark attacks do occur, fewer than 100 people have been killed by these creatures since 1791.
- Australia's highest recorded temperature is 53.1°C, measured at Cloncurry in Queensland in January 1889.
- Between 1788 and 1856, 157,000 convicts were transported to Australia.
- Surveys have revealed that Australia's top tourist activity is Sydney's shopping.

Essence of Australia

Bottom: a visit to Uluṟu (Ayers Rock) is an essential of any trip to Australia

Visitors come to Australia for many reasons, but the continent's greatest appeal is undoubtedly its 'Great Outdoors'. The climate is generally warm and balmy, the magnificent scenery includes rugged sandstone peaks and escarpments, rainforests, gleaming white sands and clear tropical waters, and the unique plants, birds and animals add an exotic touch to an already dramatic landscape.

Australia's warm climate is perfect for all types of sporting activity

There are also many historical and cultural experiences to be savoured in Australia. The locals are friendly, warm and welcoming, and this relaxed atmosphere is complemented by fabulous food and wine. A visit 'Down Under' may well surprise you with its variety of experiences.

THE 10 ESSENTIALS

If you have only a short time to visit Australia and would like to sample the very best that the continent has to offer, here are the essentials:

Dining out, especially alfresco, is enormously popular with visitors and locals alike

- **Take a cruise on Sydney Harbour** (➤ 24) and enjoy the beautiful scenery at the heart of Australia's most famous city.
- **Spend a day at the beach** to experience the sun, surf and sheer hedonism of Bondi (➤ 31) or any other of Australia's magnificent beaches. You could even have a go at surfing.
- **See a performance at the Sydney Opera House,** where you can enjoy the acclaimed Australian Ballet, Opera Australia or Sydney Symphony Orchestra inside the nation's most distinctive building (➤ 24).
- **Experience the Great Barrier Reef** – snorkel or dive among the colourful coral and luminous fish of the eighth wonder of the world (➤ 18–19).
- **Dine alfresco** to sample modern Australian cuisine, especially some of the wonderful seafood, at an outdoor table with a view across the coast.
- **Visit Uluru (Ayers Rock)** – at the very heart of the continent, the world's largest monolith exudes an awesome sense of mystery and timelessness (➤ 26).
- **Learn about Australia's history** – discover something of pre-European Aboriginal life at the Australian Museum (➤ 34), and head to Port Arthur (➤ 67) for an insight into the harsh convict days.
- **Go bushwalking** – a hike in the bush (countryside) is a must. Explore the escarpments and eucalypt forests of the Blue Mountains (➤ 23, 41).
- **Visit a wildlife park** for a close encounter with kangaroos, emus, wombats, koalas and other unique Australian fauna (➤ 35, 110).
- **Sample local wines and beers** – spend an evening in an Aussie pub, meet the locals, and enjoy world-class wines and fine beers.

Enjoy Australia's 'Great Outdoors', but remember to protect yourself from the fierce sun

The Shaping of Australia

James Cook and the crew of the Endeavour *at Botany Bay in 1770*

At least 50,000 years ago
Aborigines arrive in Australia from what is now Southeast Asia.

1606
Dutch explorer Willem Jansz sails past the Queensland coast, proving that what is known as *Terra Australis Incognita* does exist.

1770
Lieutenant James Cook and the *Endeavour* crew land at Botany Bay, south of Sydney, and later claim the eastern coast of New Holland (Australia) for King George III, under the name of New South Wales.

1779
In England, following the cessation of convict transportation to America in 1776, the first suggestions are made that New South Wales could become a penal colony.

1787
The 'First Fleet' departs from England on 13 May to sail to Botany Bay. The fleet's 11 ships carry over 1,400 people, among whom are 759 male and female convicts.

1788
The Fleet arrives in Botany Bay on 20 January. The Fleet's commander and first Governor of the colony, Captain Arthur Phillip, decides the site is unsuitable and on 26 January moves north to Port Jackson (Sydney Harbour). The colony of New South Wales is proclaimed.

1790
The Second Fleet, with a further 1,006 convicts, arrives.

1793
The first free settlers land in Sydney.

1804
Australia's second major colony is founded at Hobart, Tasmania.

1810
Scotsman Lachlan Macquarie becomes Governor and remains until 1821. During his stay, he transforms the unruly colony into a settlement with great potential and the population reaches 10,000.

1817
Governor Macquarie first refers to the colony as 'Australia' in official correspondence.

1824
Brisbane, the capital of Queensland, is founded.

1828
The first census reveals a population of 36,000 convicts and free settlers, and 2,549 military personnel.

1829
Perth and Fremantle are founded and Western Australia is proclaimed a British colony.

1832
Assisted emigration

begins – during the next 20 years over 200,000 people emigrate, mostly from Britain.

1835
The city of Melbourne is founded.

1836
The first settlers arrive in Adelaide, South Australia.

1840
Convict transportation to New South Wales ceases. A total of 83,000 convicts had been sent to the colony since 1788.

1859
Queensland, previously part of New South Wales, becomes a separate colony.

1869
Darwin, capital of the remote Northern Territory, is founded.

1901
The Commonwealth of Australia is proclaimed on 1 January, joining the six Australian colonies into a federation. Edmund Barton is elected as the first Prime Minister.

1908
Canberra is chosen as the site for the new national capital.

1923
Work begins on the construction of the Sydney Harbour Bridge, which is finally opened in 1932.

1927
The seat of national government moves from Melbourne to Canberra.

1947
Post-war immigration from Europe begins, starting the nation's slow but inexorable surge towards multiculturalism.

1966
Decimal currency, in the form of dollars and cents, replaces the old pounds, shillings and pence.

1973
Queen Elizabeth II opens the Sydney Opera House.

1975
Dismissal of the Whitlam Labor Government by the Governor General.

1988
On 26 January 200 years of European settlement are celebrated.

1996
Massacre at Port Arthur leads to strict gun control legislation.

1999
Australians vote against becoming a republic in a national referendum.

Aboriginal 'X-ray' cave painting at Nourlangie Rock in Kakadu National Park

2000
Sydney hosts the Olympic Games.

2003
Australia hosts the Rugby World Cup.

Natural Australia

Australia's 'nasties'
Some of Australia's wildlife is not quite as appealing as the much loved koala. Crocodiles inhabit the far north, sharks frequent the continent's seas, and there are many species of venomous snakes. Insect pests include mosquitoes and ants, while certain spiders – particularly the redback and the funnel-web – are to be avoided at all costs. There is no need to panic, however, as visitors are most unlikely to run into any of these 'nasties'.

It is easy to get away from it all in Australia, a vast country which – other than around the coast – is populated very sparsely. Even the large but relatively uncrowded cities offer many spots where you can find peace and quiet, with plenty of parks and gardens within their precincts. All the major cities are close to either beaches or waterways, and there is a national park virtually on the fringe of every state capital.

National Parks and World Heritage Sites

Because of its superb scenery, vast size and low population density, Australia has well over 3,000 national parks and reserves. Some of these – including Kakadu in the Northern Territory – are remote and wild; some encompass large expanses of spectacular coastline; while others, such as Sydney's magnificent Ku-ring-gai Chase, preserve unspoiled bushland and wildlife habitats just a short drive from the cities.

The 'laughing' kookaburra, a member of the kingfisher family, is one of Australia's best-known birds

Australia also has 13 UNESCO World Heritage listings, the most coveted international conservation status. Sites are included on this list for their outstanding natural or cultural significance, and Uluṟu-Kata Tjuṯa (Ayers Rock and The Olgas) and the Great Barrier Reef are among Australia's inclusions. Such unique and superbly scenic regions offer some of the continent's best natural environments and these are wonderful places to escape from the world of cities, traffic and overcrowding.

Fauna and Flora

The ancient landmass of Australia, once part of the mega-continent of Gondwana, split away from its neighbours some 50 million years ago. This long isolation has produced some extraordinary flora and fauna – much of it found nowhere else on earth – and these can be seen throughout the continent's reserves and national parks.

Australia's best-known animals are its marsupials – mammals that give birth to tiny young which go on to develop in the mother's pouch. Kangaroos, wallabies, Tasmanian devils, wombats and their closest relatives,

koalas, are all marsupials. The primitive monotremes are even more extraordinary: although mammals, the spiny echidna and the water-dwelling, billed platypus lay eggs. Reptiles include two types of crocodiles and many snakes, and Australia has a profusion of colourful and noisy birds, such as the splendidly hued lorikeet and the famous 'laughing' kookaburra.

The continent has over 15,000 flowering plant species, including 550 varieties of the classic Australian tree, the eucalyptus. This amazing plant takes many forms and can survive in climates and soils as varied as those of the southern snowfields and the central deserts. There is an incredible range of wild flowers, many of which are found nowhere else, while the far north harbours tropical rainforest so ancient and special that it is World Heritage listed.

The golden blooms of one of Western Australia's wild flowers, many of which are unique to the state

Did you know ?

Another highlight of Australia's wilderness areas is the fascinating evidence of the long Aboriginal occupation of the continent – an incredible era of survival in the most extreme conditions, spanning at least 50,000 years. In Kakadu National Park, for example, you can see superb 20,000-year-old rock art sites, while far north Queensland and Central Australia contain many other locations of indigenous cultural and artistic significance.

Australia's Famous

Errol Flynn (1909–59)
Born in Hobart, Tasmania, the legendary movie star Errol Flynn acted in his first Australian film in 1933. After moving to Hollywood in 1935, he became the epitome of the handsome, swashbuckling hero in films like *Captain Blood* and *Robin Hood*. He made over 60 films, but was equally famous for his three marriages, divorces and involvement in scandal. His 1959 autobiography was appropriately entitled *My Wicked, Wicked Ways*.

Errol Flynn: once the dashing hero of millions of movie-goers

Nicole Kidman

Born in Hawaii in 1967, Nicole moved with her family to Sydney when she was four. She became a ballet dancer and by the age of 17 had appeared in Australian films and TV series. Both her career and personal life blossomed after starring with Tom Cruise in *Days of Thunder* (1990): the couple went on to marry and make other films together, such as *Far and Away* (1992) and *Eyes Wide Shut* (1999). Since their divorce Nicole has become one of the world's most famous actors, with acclaimed performances in *Moulin Rouge* (2001) and *The Hours* (2003) for which she won an Oscar for her portrayal of Virginia Woolf.

Dame Joan Sutherland

Most of the the nation's talented classical performers are little known outside Australia, but Dame Joan Sutherland is a remarkable exception. This highly acclaimed Sydney-born opera singer made her debut at London's Covent Garden in 1952, and went on to spend 20 years there as a leading soprano. Her performances drew rave reviews in the USA and Europe, and she was given the name 'La Stupenda' by Italian audiences. Ms Sutherland was made a dame in 1979 and gave her glittering farewell performance at the Sydney Opera House in 1990.

Mel Gibson

Renowned for movies such as *The Bounty* (1984), *Hamlet* (1990) and *Maverick* (1994), Mel Gibson's laid back attitude to film-making and his approachability ensure his status as one of the mega-stars of Hollywood. Although he was born in New York in 1956, Mel grew up in Australia, where he attended drama school. He first made a name for himself in George Miller's *Mad Max* in 1979. One of his most popular roles has been the unstable Martin Riggs in the *Lethal Weapon* movies, the fourth of which was released in 1998. Mel made his directorial debut with *The Man Without a Face*, in 1996 he won an Oscar as Best Director for *Braveheart*, a movie which received four other awards, including Best Picture, and 2004 saw the release of his controversial film *The Passion of The Christ*.

Top Ten

Cairns and District	16
The Gold Coast	17
The Great Barrier Reef	18–19
Great Ocean Road	20
Kakadu National Park	21
The Kimberley	22
Blue Mountains	23
Sydney Harbour and Sydney Opera House	24
Tasmania's World Heritage Area	25
Uluru-Kata Tjuta National Park	26

Above: *Victoria's Twelve Apostles*
Right: *a Barrier Reef fish*

1

Cairns and District, North Queensland

www.tropicalaustralia.com.au

50B4

Tourism Tropical North Queensland, 51 The Esplanade, Cairns (☎ (07) 4051 3588 Daily); Port Douglas Tourist Information Centre, 23 Macrossan Street, Port Douglas (☎ (07) 4099 5599 Daily); Kuranda (☎ (07) 4093 9311)

To Cairns

Few

Inexpensive to expensive

Huge variety of accommodation from backpacker to five star. Car hire is relatively expensive but there are many bus services and tours to all popular destinations

For much of the year, tropical Cairns has the perfect climate for boating enthusiasts

Cairns is the perfect base for a superb nature-based holiday allowing trips to the World Heritage listed reefs and rainforests as well as the dry Outback.

With its international airport, well-developed tourism infrastructure and proximity to natural attractions such as the Great Barrier Reef, tropical rainforests and Atherton Tableland, Cairns is the 'tourist capital' of North Queensland. Here are dozens of hotels, restaurants and shops, and many options for cruises – as well as diving, fishing or snorkelling trips – to the reef. Excellent beaches stretch to the north and south, and adventure activities like whitewater rafting and bungee jumping are popular. Around town you can visit the Cairns Museum and the Pier Marketplace, or just wander the streets and waterfront to soak up the city's relaxed, tropical atmosphere. North of the city is the pretty coastal town of Port Douglas, while further afield are Mossman and the Daintree rainforests.

Inland from Cairns, the cool upland region of the Atherton Tableland, with its fertile farming land, volcanic lakes, waterfalls and rainforest, presents a striking contrast to the hot, humid coast. Kuranda (27km) offers colourful markets, a fauna sanctuary and rainforest interpretation centre. You can reach Kuranda by road, on the spectacular Skyrail Rainforest Cableway, or by travelling on the famous Kuranda Scenic Railway, which winds its way up the Great Dividing Range.

For a complete change, take a trip inland to the Gulf Savannah country and sample the hospitality of the Outback locals. Discover the grasslands, wetlands, escarpments and saltpans and check out the Undara Lava Tubes.

2
The Gold Coast, Queensland

Although not to everyone's liking, the brash and sometimes crass Gold Coast reveals a very different side of Australia from its natural wonders.

It would be difficult not to have a good time on this lively, highly developed 70-km strip of coastline to the south of Brisbane. Stretching down to Coolangatta on the New South Wales border, the Gold Coast offers consistently warm temperatures and an average of 300 days of sunshine each year. The sandy beaches are lapped by clear blue waters that are perfect for swimming, surfing and all kinds of water sports, and there is a smorgasbord of man-made attractions and entertainment.

The heart of the action is the appropriately named Surfers Paradise, the main town, which offers excellent shopping and dining and a host of nightlife options, including the glossy Jupiters Casino at nearby Broadbeach. Many of the Gold Coast's attractions are particularly appealing to children, and theme parks like Dreamworld, Warner Bros Movie World, Wet 'n' Wild Water World and the excellent Sea World are extremely popular. There are many fine golf courses in the area, you can take a cruise to tranquil South Stradbroke Island, go water-skiing, or even sample the daredevil sport of bungee jumping. The Coast's list of things to do is almost endless.

If you prefer to stay somewhere quieter, however, the southern area around Coolangatta offers a less frenetic pace – and fewer high-rise buildings. This is also the location for Currumbin Wildlife Sanctuary. When you've had enough of the coast, a short trip to the hinterland, particularly to Lamington National Park (▶ 53) or the delightful mountain town of Mount Tamborine, is a rewarding experience. Excellent scenery and a cooler environment, with rainforest walking tracks and a diversity of art and craft shops, make this town a great day trip.

www.goldcoasttourism.com.au

51D1

Gold Coast Tourism Bureau, Cavill Avenue, Surfers Paradise (☎ (07) 5538 4419 Mon–Fri 8:30–5:30, Sat 9–5, Sun 9–3:30)

To Coolangatta

Coach transfers (from Brisbane)

Gold Coast (from Brisbane)

Along with its high-rises and tourist development, the Gold Coast offers wonderful beaches and excellent surf

3
The Great Barrier Reef, Queensland

www.gbrmpa.gov.au
www.queenslandholidays.com
www.queenslandtravel.com

51C3

Queensland Travel Centre, 30 Makerston Street, Brisbane (☎ (07) 3874 2800, fax (07) 3221 5320 Mon–Fri 8:30–5)

Proserpine, Townsville, Cairns

To Proserpine, Townsville, Cairns

The Great Barrier Reef is often described as the eighth wonder of the world, and a visit to this marine wonderland will be long remembered.

Running parallel to the Queensland coast for over 2,000km – from Papua New Guinea to just south of the Tropic of Capricorn – the Great Barrier Reef is the world's largest living structure. This extraordinary ecosystem is, in fact, made of over 2,000 linked reefs and around 700 islands and fringing reefs, and is composed of and built by countless tiny coral polyps and algae. This famous natural attraction is protected by its Great Barrier Reef Marine Park status and World Heritage listing.

The reef itself is home to many different types of coral: some are brightly coloured, while others, like the aptly-named staghorns, take on strange formations. The reef's tropical waters host an incredible variety of marine life – everything from tiny, luminously coloured fish to sharks, manta rays, turtles and dolphins. There are many ways to

view and explore this fabulous underwater world: scenic flights, boat trips, snorkelling or scuba diving, and glass-bottom or semi-submersible boat trips.

For the very best Great Barrier Reef experience, it is possible to stay right on the reef. The idyllic coral cays of Green Island, Heron Island and Lady Elliot Island offer resort accommodation, while Lady Musgrave is for campers only. Other options are to base yourself at a coastal resort (Townsville, Cairns and Port Douglas in the north, or the Whitsunday Islands further south are the best bets) or on one of the many non-reef islands. Some island suggestions are Lizard, Dunk and Magnetic Island in the north; Hayman, South Molle and Hamilton in the Whitsunday region; and Great Keppel Island in the south.

The wonders of the Great Barrier Reef:
Above: *a close underwater encounter*
Left: *Green Island, a true coral cay*

4
Great Ocean Road, Victoria

www.greatoceanrd.org.au

60B1

Geelong and Great Ocean Road Visitor Centre, Princes Highway, Geelong (1800 620 888 (toll free) or (03) 5275 5797 Daily 9–5. Closed 25 Dec)

None: driving is recommended

West Coast Railway to Warrnambool only

Ballarat (► 63)

The Great Ocean Road encompasses some of Australia's most dramatic coastal scenery

A journey along Australia's most spectacular road reveals superb coastal scenery, charming old resorts and fishing villages, and a forested hinterland.

Extending from Torquay to Port Fairy, Victoria's Great Ocean Road snakes its way along the state's south-west coast for a distance of 300km. Geelong, 75km from Melbourne, is a good starting point and nearby Bells Beach, one of Australia's surfing meccas, is a good spot to get in the mood for this oceanside drive.

The quiet holiday village of Anglesea is famous for the kangaroos which roam the local golf course, while Lorne offers fine beaches, a delightful seaside resort atmosphere, and forested hillsides inland. Beyond here lies the fishing town of Apollo Bay and magnificent Otway National Park – an irresistible combination of rugged coastline and lush inland rainforest.

The coast becomes more dramatic as you reach Port Campbell National Park. This much photographed coastline is the result of erosion caused by wind, rain and the stormy Southern Ocean – a process which has created spectacular formations. The picturesque town of Port Campbell, with its port, historical museum and self-guided heritage trail, is the ideal base for exploring this very special area.

Further west along this wild coastline, the aptly named Shipwreck Coast is famous for the migrating whales which give birth here between May and August each year, while the town of Warrnambool offers the interesting Flagstaff Hill Maritime Museum, a re-created 19th-century village. The Great Ocean Road proper ends at the charming fishing village of Port Fairy, where there are over 50 National Trust listed buildings, beaches and coastal cruises to enjoy.

5

Kakadu National Park, Northern Territory

Australia's largest national park is both a superb tropical wilderness and a treasure house of ancient Aboriginal art and culture.

Contrasts of Kakadu – blue sky, rugged cliffs, and a waterhole

Covering almost 20,000sq km to the east of Darwin, this vast World Heritage registered national park is one of Australia's most spectacular attractions. Much of Kakadu is a flat, river-crossed floodplain that is transformed into a lake during the wet season, but this large area is backed by forested lowlands, hills, and the dramatic 250-m cliffs of the Arnhem Land escarpment. The extraordinary wildlife within this varied terrain ranges from dangerous estuarine crocodiles to dingoes, wallabies, snakes, goannas and over 280 species of bird.

There is much evidence of the area's long Aboriginal occupation, which may have endured for an incredible 50,000 years. Aboriginal-owned Kakadu includes Nourlangie and Ubirr rocks, where you can see fine examples of Aboriginal painting, estimated to be around 20,000 years old. Among the park's scenic highlights are the spectacular Jim Jim Falls and Twin Falls that tumble off the escarpment, and Yellow Water – a tranquil waterhole and wetlands area, home to prolific birdlife.

During the Top End's wet season (November to April) many of the roads are impassable, so the best time to visit Kakadu is during the 'Dry' – from May to October. Much of the park can be explored in a normal vehicle, but a four-wheel drive is necessary for off-road travelling. General information is available from the main Visitor Centre, but the Warradjan Aboriginal Cultural Centre at Yellow Water provides a deeper insight into the area's indigenous culture and history. To see something of modern Aboriginal life, you can visit neighbouring Arnhem Land; this is Aboriginal land and permits are required to visit, so a tour is the only real option.

www.deh.gov.au/parks
www.ntholidays.com

78B5

Bowali Visitor Centre, Kakadu Highway
(08) 8938 1120
Daily 8–5)

Cafés in the area (£–££)

To Jabiru

Moderate

Guided walks and tours from Visitor Centre

6
The Kimberley, Western Australia

www.kimberleytourism.com

28B4

West Kimberley Tourist Bureau, Broome Highway/Bagot Road, Broome; East Kimberley Tourist Bureau, Coolibah Drive, Kununurra; Broome Tourist Bureau (☎ (08) 9192 2222, fax (08) 9192 2063); Kununurra Tourist Bureau (☎ (08) 9168 1177, fax (08) 9168 2598 Daily, generally 9–4)

To Broome or Kununurra

Best visited Apr–Oct, and rental of a four-wheel drive vehicle is recommended. Purnululu National Park closed Jan–Mar

In the far north of Western Australia, the Kimberley is one of the continent's remotest and most spectacular regions.

Explored and settled as late as the 1880s, the Kimberley is extremely rugged and very sparsely settled – the population of just 25,000 lives in Aboriginal settlements, on enormous cattle stations, and in a few small towns. This vast region of 420,000sq km is generally divided into two main areas, the West and East Kimberley.

The tropical town of Broome, with its multicultural population, pearl history and fabulous beaches, is the ideal starting point for exploring the western region. The nearby settlement of Derby has an interesting Royal Flying Doctor Service base, while inland attractions include the dramatic Geikie Gorge National Park, with its 14km-long gorge.

You can reach the East Kimberley by driving north and east from Broome or flying to Kununurra, a town near the Northern Territory border and the base for the ambitious 1960s and 1970s Ord River Irrigation Scheme. This project

An early sunset over the East Kimberley highlights the rock formations and casts dramatic shadows

created the vast Argyle and Kununurra lakes – welcome breaks in the otherwise arid landscape. From here you can visit the Argyle Diamond Mine, then travel north to the remote port of Wyndham, or south to the wondrous Bungle Bungles. Contained within Purnululu National Park, 'discovered' only in 1983, and given World Heritage status in 2003, these spectacular rock formations, up to 300m high, are composed of extremely friable striped silica and sandstone eroded into beehive-like shapes.

Other attractions worth seeing in this wild, last-frontier landscape include the Aboriginal rock art sites of Mirima National Park near Kununurra; Windjana Gorge National Park, reached via the small town of Fitzroy Crossing; and the amazing Wolfe Creek Crater – an enormous depression created by a meteorite.

7

Blue Mountains, New South Wales

For a complete change to Sydney's glamour, visit these nearby mountains to experience the great natural beauty of their geological wonders.

This is one of Australia's most popular holiday destinations. Visitors come to the Blue Mountains to experience their wild grandeur, mist-filled valleys, rich Aboriginal and European heritage, and to escape the summer heat. The cold winters allow visitors to enjoy the charm of open fires. Just two hours by road or train from Sydney, the mountains get their name from their blue haze.

There is so much to do and see here, from just taking in the panoramic views from the many escarpment lookouts to walking in the temperate rainforests which line the ravines and valleys. Waterfalls cascade off the cliffs into valleys far below, where they join streams that disappear into dense vegetation. The golden brown of ancient, weathered rockfaces, formed by the action of the elements over millions of years, contrasts with the distinctive blue green of the mountain vegetation.

Because of the great range and diversity of land forms and plant communities, and its habitats sheltering rare or endangered fauna, the Greater Blue Mountains region became a World Heritage Site in 2000. In addition to its natural sights and adventure sports, there are myriad galleries, antique shops, gardens, museums and fine eating establishments to enjoy. The Katoomba Scenic Railway and the Sceniscender provide unique perspectives of their surroundings while just over the range are the famous Jenolan Caves with their amazing limestone formations.

www.bluemountainstourism.org

39E2

From Sydney to most locations; driving is another option

Information Centres, Great Western Highway, Glenbrook (1300 653 408) Echo Point, Katoomba ((02) 4782 9865) Glenbrook: Mon–Fri 9–5, Sat–Sun 8:30–4:30. Closed 25 Dec;

Few

A wide range of accommodation from B&Bs to five star. Many tour companies operate day tours from Sydney

The entire Blue Mountains region is heavily timbered with eucalypts which constantly disperse droplets of oil into the air, causing the blue rays from the sun to be scattered more effectively, which makes distant objects appear blue

8
Sydney Harbour & Sydney Opera House

www.sydneyopera house.com

33B5

Sydney Opera House: Bennelong Point

Sydney Opera House: (02) 9250 7250 for tours; (02) 9250 7777 for details of performances

Sydney Opera House: guided tours 8:30–5 on most days

Good

Moderate–Expensive

Guillaume at Bennelong restaurant (£££), cafés (£–££)

Circular Quay

Mrs Macquaries Point, The Domain and Royal Botanic Gardens (➤ 36)

Markets on Sun

A classic Australian scene – Sydney's beautiful harbour, graced by its world-famous Opera House and Harbour Bridge

Complemented by the ethereal, sail-like outlines of the famous Opera House, Sydney Harbour is the glittering jewel of Australia's most exciting city.

From the day in January 1788 when the 11 convict-bearing ships of the First Fleet sailed into Port Jackson, Sydney's harbour has been the focus of this great city. A harbour cruise – be it on a luxury boat or a humble Sydney ferry – is a must. From the water you will see the city, including the large areas of bushland of the Sydney Harbour National Park, from a new perspective. Ferries are also the best way to reach waterfront suburbs and the harbour's delightful beaches. From Circular Quay you can take a trip to the beaches of Manly on the north side of the harbour, or to the charming southside suburb of Watsons Bay, close to the harbour's entrance. Ferries also visit some of the national park's islands, including historic Fort Denison.

On the harbour's southern shore, the curved roofs of the Sydney Opera House soar above Bennelong Point. Completed in 1973, after 14 years and many technical and political problems, this architectural masterpiece, designed by Dane Joern Utzon, still inspires controversy. There is no doubt, however, that the structure's stone platform and dramatic white roofs, covered with over a million ceramic tiles, have made it one of the world's most distinctive buildings. Once you have inspected the exterior, attending a performance or taking a guided tour of the five performance halls is highly recommended. Looming above the magnificent harbour is the third ingredient of this classic Sydney scene – the grand old Sydney Harbour Bridge, completed in 1932 and, with a tunnel opened in 1992, still the major link between the south and north shores (➤ 35).

9
Tasmania's World Heritage Area

Much of the island of Tasmania is superb wilderness, and the state's relatively small size means these untouched areas are easily accessible.

Tasmania's wilderness is of such significant natural beauty that around 20 per cent – an incredible 1.38 million hectares – of the state is under World Heritage protection. This land of rugged peaks, wild rivers, moorland and remote coastline also contains many sites of Aboriginal significance, while the wildlife includes Tasmanian devils, echidnas and the elusive platypus.

One of the most accessible regions in the World Heritage Area is the Cradle Mountain-Lake St Clair National Park, just 170km from the capital, Hobart. The alpine scenery here is truly spectacular – high peaks that include Mount Ossa (1,617m), the state's highest mountain, lakes, alpine moorlands and rainforests. There are many hiking tracks here, the most famous of which is the five to ten day Overland Track in the heart of the Cradle Mountain-Lake St Clair National Park.

To the south, the Franklin-Gordon Wild Rivers National Park is particularly famous for its adventurous Franklin River whitewater rafting. Even more remote and untamed wilderness is found in the Southwest National Park, the domain of forests, lakes and a long, deeply indented coastline. Experienced hikers will enjoy the challenge of this park's 85km South Coast Track. Much closer to Hobart and characterised by its heathlands and rugged dolerite ranges, is the Hartz Mountains National Park.

November to April are the best months to go, but the weather can be unpredictable at any time, changing in minutes from warm and sunny to rain, or even snow.

www.dpiwe.tas.gov.au

64B3

Tasmanian Parks and Wildlife Service, 134 Macquarie Street, Hobart (☎ (03) 6233 6191 Mon–Fri 9–5)

From Hobart, Devonport and Launceston to some locations; driving is the best option

To Southwest National Park

Few

Parks: inexpensive

Hobart, Launceston, Strahan (➤ 64–67)

A winter scene in Tasmania – Cradle Mountain and Dove Lake, part of the World Heritage Area

10
Uluṟu-Kata Tjuṯa National Park, Northern Territory

www.deh.gov.au/parks
www.voyages.com.au

78A1

Visitors Centre, Ayers Rock Resort (☎ (08) 8957 7377 ⊙ Daily 9–5:30)

Cafés and restaurants in the area (£–££)

Ayers Rock Resort

Few

Park entry fee: moderate

Watarrka National Park (➤ 80)

Tour and information centre (☎ (08) 8957 7324 ⊙ Daily 8AM–8:30PM)

This 1,325-hectare World Heritage Site incorporates two of Australia's most spectacular sights – Uluṟu, better known as Ayers Rock, and neighbouring Kata Tjuṯa (The Olgas).

Located at the centre of the continent, Uluṟu's vast bulk is an extraordinary and overwhelming sight. At 348m high and with a base circumference of some 9km, this is the world's largest monolith – a massive rock which is made even more dramatic by its setting on the monotonous plains of the Red Centre. Uluṟu was first sighted by Europeans in 1872, but this area has been sacred to the local Aboriginal people for tens of thousands of years. It is possible to climb the rock, but this can be dangerous and the activity is discouraged by Uluṟu's Aboriginal landowners. Other options are to take a hiking tour of the base, and to view the monolith at sunset, when its normally dark red colour changes dramatically as the light fades.

Although, like Uluṟu, it is the tip of a vast underground formation, Kata Tjuṯa, 30km to the west, offers a rather different experience. The name means 'many heads' – an appropriate description of the 30 or so massive rocks which make up The Olgas. There are several trails among the formation's gorges and valleys, although most should be undertaken only if you are well prepared.

A visit to the Uluṟu-Kata Tjuṯa Cultural Centre, just a kilometre from Uluṟu, is a must. This excellent complex includes displays on Aboriginal culture and history, demonstrations of traditional art and dance, and a shop that sells local arts and crafts. The base for exploring the national park is the well-designed Ayers Rock Resort village.

Rising dramatically from the surrounding plains, 348m-high Uluṟu is simply awe-inspiring

What To See

New South Wales	30–43
Food and Drink	44–5
Queensland	46–55
Victoria and Tasmania	56–67
In the Know	68–9
South Australia and Northern Territory	70–81
Western Australia	82–90

Above: *camping in the Outback*
Right: *Sydney Explorer bus stop*

AUSTRALIA
RI
Melville Island
DARWIN
ARNHE
Daly
Cape Londonderry
Joseph Bonaparte Gulf
Katherine
Wyndham
Kununurra
KIMBERLEY
Derby
Broome
Fitzroy Crossing
Halls Creek
NORT
Tanami Desert
Great Sandy Desert
Port Hedland
Dampier
Lake Mackay
TERR
MacDonne
PILBARA
Ashburton
Lake Disappointment
Newman
Gibson Desert
Yulara
Uluru (Ayers Rock)
WESTERN
Gascoyne
Carnarvon
Lake Carnegie
Musgrave Range
Meekatharra
AUSTRALIA
Great Victoria Desert
AU
Geraldton
Lake Barlee
Kalgoorlie
Nullarbor Plain
Norseman
PERTH
Great Australian Big
Bunbury
Esperance
Cape Leeuwin
Albany
0 200 400 600 800 km
A
B
C
1
2
3
4
5
95
94

Torres Strait
Cape York
PNG
Cape Wessel
Cape Arnhem
LAND
Groote Eylandt
Weipa
Cape York Peninsula
Gulf of Carpentaria
Borroloola
Wellesley Islands
Great Barrier Reef
Cairns
Normanton
Great Dividing Range
Tennant Creek
Cloncurry
Charters Towers
Townsville
Mount Isa
Mackay
QUEENSLAND
Winton
Boulia
Alice Springs
Warburton
Longreach
Emerald
Rockhampton
Simpson Desert
Great Artesian Basin
Biloela
Gladstone
Bundaberg
Fraser Island
Maryborough
Quilpie
Charleville
Lake Eyre
Cooper Creek
Toowoomba
BRISBANE
Dirranbandi
Flinders Range
Bourke
Moree
Glen Innes
Grafton
Darling
Broken Hill
Nyngan
Tamworth
Port Augusta
NEW SOUTH WALES
Dubbo
Port Macquarie
Whyalla
Port Pirie
Bathurst
Newcastle
Port Lincoln
Spencer Gulf
Mildura
Hay
SYDNEY
Wollongong
ADELAIDE
Murray
Wagga Wagga
Albury
CANBERRA
Kangaroo Island
2228m
Snowy Mts
AUSTRALIAN CAPITAL TERRITORY
VICTORIA
Mount Gambier
Ballarat
Geelong
MELBOURNE
Cape Howe
Warrnambool
Wilsons Promontory
King Island
Bass Strait
Flinders Island
Burnie
Launceston
Queenstown
TASMANIA
HOBART
South East Cape
D
E
F
1
66
78
71
54
39
15
32
75
20
8
79
87

New South Wales

New South Wales, named by Cook in 1770 because it reminded him of south Wales, is Australia's fourth-largest state but has the largest population – almost 6.7 million. Geographically, it is made up of a series of parallel strips: a narrow coastal plain which supports the bulk of the population, the uplands of the Great Dividing Range, slopes and plains which form the state's agricultural heartland and, finally, the Outback. The climate varies from subtropical in the north to the winter snows of the mountains in the far south. Although within the boundaries of New South Wales, the Australian Capital Territory is governed and administered separately. The territory and the national capital, Canberra, were created early this century to resolve the long-running rivalry between Sydney and Melbourne over which city should be the nation's capital.

'... few cities on earth have arrived at so agreeable a fulfilment ... they are very lucky people, whose fates have washed them up upon this brave and generally decent shore.'

JAN MORRIS ON SYDNEY
Among the Cities (1983)

Sydney

The nation's birthplace has developed from its humble convict beginnings into a vibrant metropolis that holds its own on the world stage. With a multicultural population of over 4 million, Sydney is the continent's largest and, many would say, most brash, city. Although the pace of life is faster here than anywhere else in Australia, Sydneysiders still know how to relax – the city's harbour, long golden beaches and surrounding bushland make sure of that.

Sydney has it all – a modern, upbeat city centre, harbour and waterfront and a relaxing way of life

In recent years Sydney has truly come of age as a major city and an enviable tourist destination. It has been voted 'the world's best city' by discerning travellers the world over, but perhaps the biggest accolade of all came when Sydney was chosen as the host city for the 2000 Summer Olympic Games. There is plenty to see and do: in addition to the fascinating convict history, museums, galleries and, of course, the 'Great Outdoors', the city offers wonderful shopping, an innovative and highly acclaimed restaurant scene and a wide choice of nightlife.

Although visitors spend most of their time in the inner city and eastern suburbs, an entirely different world lies beyond. To the north lie the glorious Northern Beaches with surf, sand and a far more relaxed lifestyle, the charming waterway of Pittwater, and the bushland of Ku-ring-gai Chase National Park. To the west, you can visit historic Parramatta and Sydney Olympic Park, the Olympic Games site. Sydney's inner suburbs also have a great deal to offer. A visit to famous Bondi, Manly or one of the many other beaches is a must.

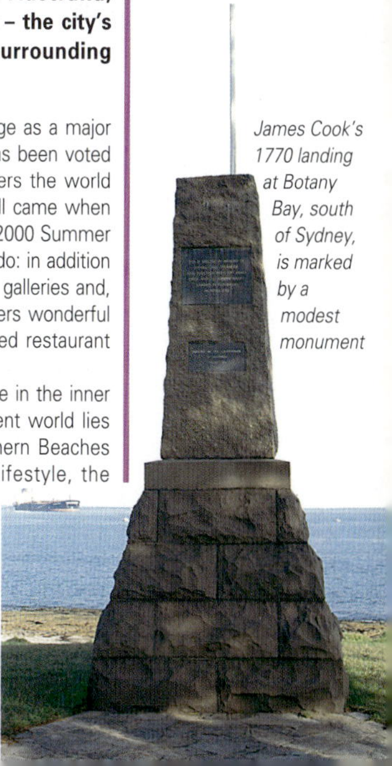

James Cook's 1770 landing at Botany Bay, south of Sydney, is marked by a modest monument

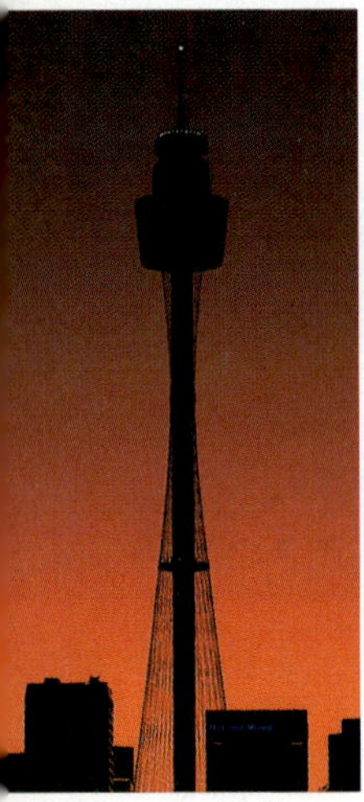

The telecommunications tower (Sydney Tower) at night; Australia's tallest building affords brilliant views of the city and its surroundings

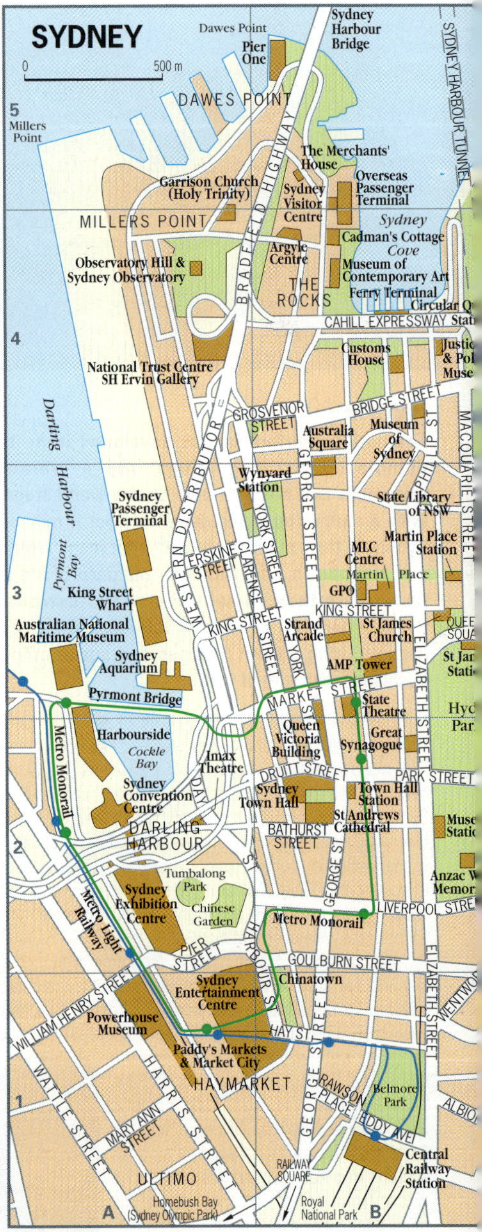

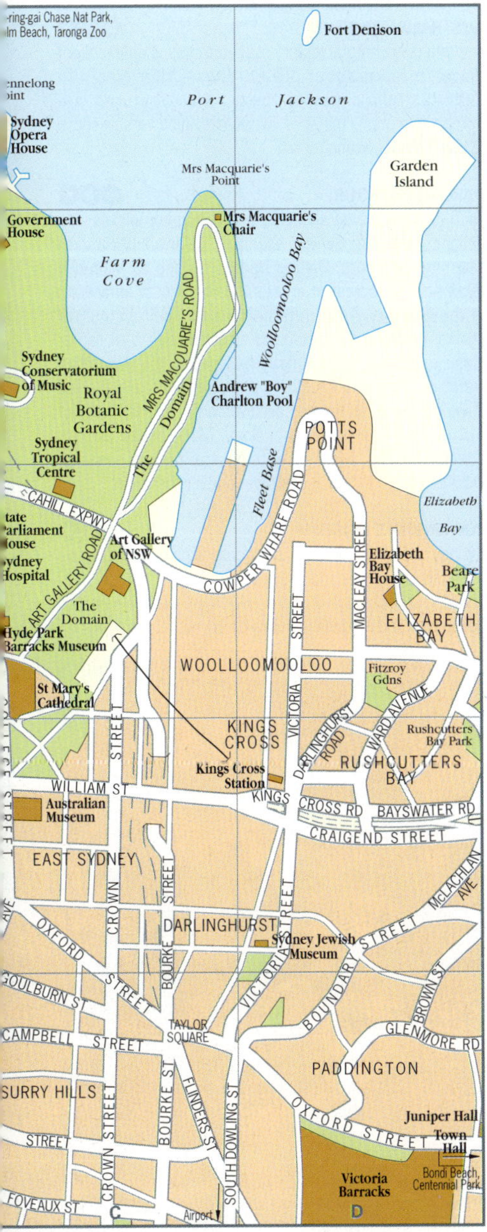

Dazzling fireworks in Sydney on Australia Day

What to See in Sydney

33C2
6 College Street
(02) 9320 6000
Daily 9:30–5. Closed 25 Dec
Moderate

AUSTRALIAN MUSEUM ✪✪✪

A world-class natural history museum, this is an excellent place to learn about pre-European Aboriginal life and Australia's native fauna. Also featured are human evolution, minerals, dinosaurs, biodiversity and a fascinating skeletons room.

www.darlingharbour.com
32A3
Darling Harbour
1902 260 568 or (02) 9281 0788
Daily 9:30–5:30
Excellent
Sydney Aquarium
(02) 9262 2300
Daily 9AM–10PM (last admission at 8)
Monorail to Darling Park
Very good
Expensive

DARLING HARBOUR ✪✪✪

With its harbourside shopping and eating complexes, the delightful Chinese Garden, the Imax Theatre and National Maritime Museum, Darling Harbour is one of Sydney's most popular recreation areas. One of the best attractions is the **Sydney Aquarium**, where you will encounter sharks, crocodiles and colourful Great Barrier Reef fish at close quarters. The futuristic building of the Australian National Maritime Museum contains several galleries covering maritime themes as diverse as the discovery of Australia and surfboard technology. Many of the exhibits are interactive. Moored outside are various vessels, including a World War II destroyer and a submarine.

32A1
500 Harris Street, Ultimo
(02) 9217 0111
Daily 10–5. Closed 25 Dec
Moderate

POWERHOUSE MUSEUM ✪✪

Sydney's largest museum is an entertaining technological and cultural wonderland with everything from a huge 18th-century steam engine and a 1930s art deco cinema to holograms and irresistible hands-on computer displays.

Right: *Darling Harbour's beautifully designed Chinese Garden provides a tranquil oasis in the heart of the city*

Facing page: *an unusual view of the Sydney Harbour Bridge from the harbour's north shore*

THE ROCKS ✪✪✪

With its intriguing past and prime harbourside location, this is Sydney's tourist mecca. The Rocks was the site of Australia's first 'village', and the region has had a colourful history. In addition to wandering the narrow streets, sitting on the waterfront and browsing in the many shops, Rocks highlights are a lively weekend market and several small museums – including the Sydney Observatory at nearby Millers Point. Full details of the area are available from the Information Centre.

www.sydneyvisitorcentre.com
- 32B4
- Sydney Visitor Centre, 106 George Street
- (02) 9240 8788
- Daily 9:30–5:30, closed 25 Dec and Good Fri
- Circular Quay
- Free

SYDNEY HARBOUR (➤ 24, TOP TEN)

SYDNEY HARBOUR BRIDGE ✪✪

Completed in 1932, this famous bridge is still the primary link between the harbour's north and south shores, although the Sydney Harbour Tunnel now handles a large share of the traffic. You can inspect the bridge from close up by taking the walkway from the Rocks, and then climbing the 200 steps of the Pylon. For really spectacular views of the harbour and city, take the BridgeClimb tour.

- 32B5
- Pylon Lookout (02) 9247 3408; BridgeClimb (02) 8274 7777
- Pylon Lookout and Museum daily 10–5. Closed 25 Dec
- Circular Quay and a walk
- None
- Lookout inexpensive; BridgeClimb expensive

SYDNEY OPERA HOUSE (➤ 24, TOP TEN)

SYDNEY TOWER ✪✪✪

The best view in town is from the top of this 304.8-m tower. From the observation level there are superb 360-degree views of the city and its surrounds. The tower has two revolving restaurants, particularly spectacular at night.

- 32B3
- 100 Market Street
- (02) 9223 0933
- Sun–Fri 9AM–10:30PM, Sat 9AM–11:30PM

TARONGA ZOO ✪✪

Reached by a scenic ferry ride, Taronga is visited as much for its harbourside location as for the opportunity to meet native Australian wildlife. All the well-known marsupials and monotremes – including koalas, kangaroos, echidnas, wombats and Tasmanian devils – are here, as well as indigenous birds and reptiles, and a large collection of exotic creatures like Sumatran tigers and elephants.

- Off map
- Bradleys Head Road, Mosman
- (02) 9969 2777
- Daily 9–5, closed 25 Dec
- Cafés (££) and kiosk (£)
- Good
- Expensive

Opera House, Royal Botanic Gardens & Macquarie Street

Distance
3km

Time
2–4 hours, depending on Opera House and museum visits

Start/end point
Circular Quay
32B4
Circular Quay

Lunch
Botanic Gardens Restaurant and Kiosk (£–££)
Royal Botanic Gardens
(02) 9241 2419

This enjoyable walk combines a harbour foreshore stroll with visits to an art gallery and some historic buildings.

Start at Circular Quay.

Lively Circular Quay is the focus of the city's ferry system. There are many cafés in the area, which is famous for its offbeat entertainers.

Follow the Circular Quay East walkway towards the Opera House.

Inspect the exterior of Australia's most famous building, then take a guided tour of the performance halls.

Enter the Botanic Gardens via the gate near the Opera House.

Sydney's waterfront Royal Botanic Gardens contain an outstanding collection of native and imported flora. The lush Sydney Tropical Centre is one of the highlights here.

The historic buildings of Sydney's Rocks area (foreground) contrast with the modern high-rises that surround Circular Quay

After exploring the gardens, continue around the foreshore to the eastern side of the cove.

From the headland known as Mrs Macquaries Point there are classic views of Sydney Harbour, the Opera House and the Harbour Bridge.

Head south along Mrs Macquaries Road until you reach the Art Gallery.

The Art Gallery of New South Wales is the state's premier gallery, with superb examples of Australian, Aboriginal, European and Asian art. By the gallery is The Domain, a large parkland area.

Follow Art Gallery Road until you reach College Street, then turn right.

Gracious Macquarie Street contains many historic buildings, including the 1819 Hyde Park Barracks, once a home for convicts but now a fascinating museum, and State Parliament House, dating from 1816.

Continue along Macquarie Street, then turn left into Albert Street to return to Circular Quay.

What to See in New South Wales

A stretch of sandy coastline near Coffs Harbour

BLUE MOUNTAINS (➤ 23, TOP TEN)

BROKEN HILL ✪

This harsh sunbaked land is another world, far removed from Sydney's waterside ambience. The silver-mining town of Broken Hill, in the far west, is a good Outback destination. Here you can tour one of the mines, visit the Royal Flying Doctor Service base, and take a trip to nearby Kinchega National Park, or the ghost town of Silverton.

www.murrayoutback.org.au
- 38A3
- Broken Hill Visitor Centre, Blende Street (☎ (08) 8087 6077 ⏲ Daily 8.30–5. Closed 25 Dec)
- Broken Hill
- From Sydney

BYRON BAY ✪✪

Paradise for beach lovers, with golden sand, a wonderful climate, clear blue water and pounding surf, 'Byron' attracts surfers, scuba divers and holidaymakers in droves. You can walk to Cape Byron (mainland Australia's most easterly point), enjoy fine restaurants, or just browse around the many art and craft shops. Take a drive to the hinterland rainforests or the small town of Mullumbimby.

www.visitbyronbay.com
- 39F5
- Byron Bay Visitor Centre, 80 Jonson Street (☎ (02) 6680 8558 ⏲ Daily 9–5. Closed 25 Dec)
- Ballina or Lismore, then a drive

COFFS HARBOUR ✪✪

Tourism and banana growing are the main industries of this north-coast city, which offers excellent beaches and a warm, sunny climate. Other attractions include the Big Banana leisure park and the Pet Porpoise Pool, while a drive inland to the picturesque upland town of Bellingen and the rainforests of World Heritage-listed Dorrigo National Park is highly recommended.

www.coffscoast.com.au
- 39F4
- Coffs Coast Visitor Centre, Corner of Elizabeth & Maclean streets (☎ (02) 6652 1522 ⏲ Daily 9–5. Closed Good Fri, 25 Dec)

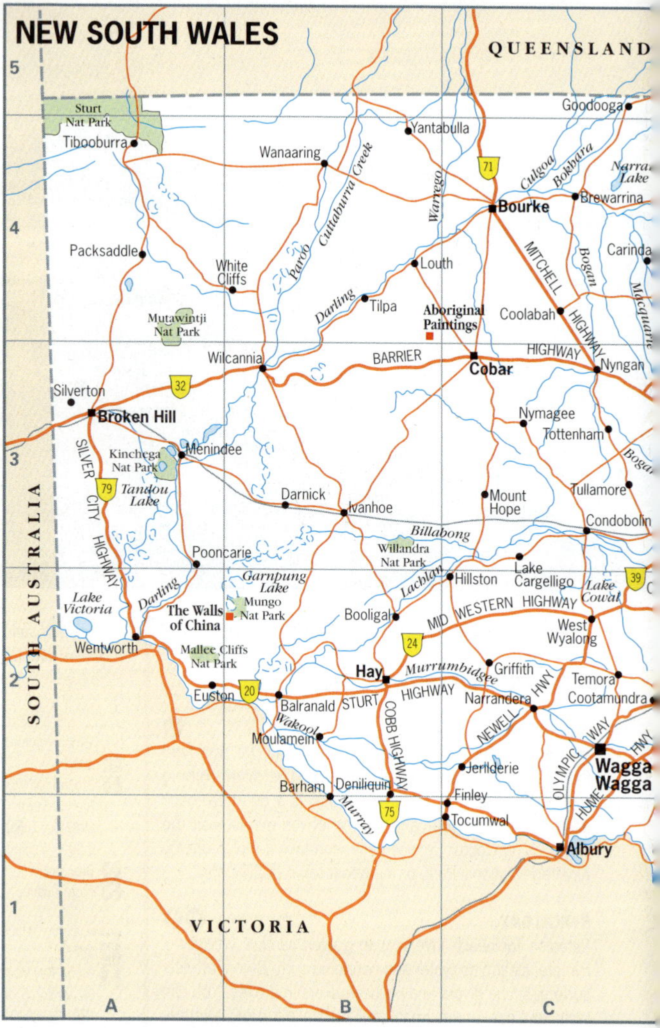

www.wineclountry.com.au
39E3
Hunter Valley Wine Country Visitor Centre, main Road, Pokolbin (02) 4990 4477 Mon–Fri 9–5, Sat 9:30–5, Sun 9:30–3:30
Maitland, then a bus to Cessnock

HUNTER VALLEY

Wine and wineries are the main attraction of this large river valley northwest of Sydney, centred around the town of Cessnock and the village of Pokolbin. Grapes have been cultivated here since the 1830s and there are now over 100 wineries in the region; many of these can be toured and you can, of course, sample the fine wines that originate from the area. The Hunter also has a reputation for excellent accommodation and dining, making it a very popular weekend destination for Sydneysiders.

KIAMA ✪✪

One of the closest South Coast seaside resorts to Sydney, just a 90-minute drive, the small town of Kiama has long enjoyed great popularity. As well as good beaches and surfing, the town has a famous blowhole, discovered by whaler George Bass in 1797 on a voyage of coastal exploration, and many historic buildings.

Inland, Kiama is close to the charmingly rural Kangaroo Valley, and the Minnamurra Rainforest Centre within the Budderoo National Park.

www.kiama.com.au

39E2

Kiama Visitor Centre, Blowhole Point Road (☎ (02) 4232 3322 Daily 9–5. Closed 25 Dec)

Kiama

www.lordhoweisland.info
Off map
Lord Howe Island Tourist Centre (☎ (02) 9244 1777); Island Visitors Centre (☎ (02) 6563 2114 Mon–Fri 9–4, Sun 9–12:30)
From Sydney and Brisbane

LORD HOWE ISLAND ✪✪

A true South Sea paradise. Dominated by sheer peaks this World Heritage-listed small island is just 11km long and 2.8km at its widest. The high peaks and lower, scattered hills were created by volcanic activity, and below these lie Kentia palm forests, idyllic sandy beaches, a fringing coral reef, and the clear blue waters of the island's lagoon, home to over 500 fish species. Visitors are well catered for with various grades of accommodation.

www.nationalparks.nsw.gov.au
39E3
☎ (02) 4984 8200
Daily Few
Inexpensive
No public transport into the park

MYALL LAKES NATIONAL PARK ✪

This North Coast national park encompasses both a chain of large freshwater lakes and an idyllic 40km coastline. You can hire a houseboat or canoe to explore the lakes, or camp and enjoy surfing and swimming off the golden beaches. The area is particularly appealing to birdwatchers and bushwalkers.

39D1
Kosciuszko National Park
Snowy Region Visitor Centre, Kosciuszko Road, Jindabyne
☎ (02) 6450 5600
Daily, winter 8–5:30; summer 8:30–5
Jindabyne and Thredbo. Perisher Blue (ski season)

SNOWY MOUNTAINS ✪✪

In the state's far south, reached via the town of Jindabyne, this upland region encompasses **Kosciuszko National Park**, where you can ski in winter from the resorts of Thredbo and Perisher Blue. The wilderness park contains heathland and alpine vegetation, as well as Mount Kosciuszko, Australia's highest point (just 2,228m). In summer the area is great for bushwalking, trout fishing, horse riding and mountain biking.

www.southern-highlands. com.au
39D2
Information Centre, 62–70 Main Street, Mittagong (☎ (02) 4871 2888 Daily 8–5:30)
Mittagong, Bowral, Moss Vale, Exeter, Bundanoon

SOUTHERN HIGHLANDS ✪✪✪

Just 100km from Sydney, this upland region offers a blend of rugged Australian bush, rolling English-type farmland and genteel townships.

Colonial history is well represented: the charming village of Berrima dates from the early 1830s and is full of historic buildings. You can shop for crafts and antiques in Berrima, Moss Vale and Bowral, and go bushwalking in the Morton National Park.

The Blue Mountains

This drive takes you to one of Sydney's favourite recreation areas – the rugged and scenic Blue Mountains.

From central Sydney, go west along Parramatta Road, to join the Western Motorway (M4). Continue on to the Great Western Highway (Route 32) at the base of the mountains.

After Glenbrook (information centre), continue to the Norman Lindsay Gallery and Museum at Faulconbridge, devoted to one of Australia's most celebrated artists and writers. Wentworth Falls offers short bushwalks and the Falls Reserve.

Continue on the highway until you reach the Leura turnoff.

The picturesque town of Leura has cafés, crafts shops and the cool-climate Everglades Gardens.

Take the signposted scenic Cliff Drive to nearby Katoomba.

This brings you to Echo Point with spectacular views of the Three Sisters, the surrounding cliffs, and the forested Jamison Valley.

Continue on the Cliff Drive, which rejoins the Great Western Highway. Follow the signs to Blackheath.

In Blackheath, head for the National Parks and Wildlife Service Heritage Centre, and a splendid panorama.

Keep following the Great Western Highway to Mount Victoria.

Mount Victoria is classifed as an Urban Conservation Area and has a museum, teashops and a few antique shops.

Follow the Darling Causeway then turn right on to the Bells Line of Road.

Visit Mount Tomah Botanic Garden, the cool-climate branch of Sydney's Royal Botanic Gardens.

Continue to Windsor, then follow Route 40, and the Western Motorway.

Distance
280km

Time
A full day, or stay overnight if possible

Start/end point
George Street, central Sydney
32B2

Lunch
Café Bon Ton (£–££)
192 The Mall, Leura
(02) 4782 4377

Above: *the famous Three Sisters rock formation from Echo Point near Katoomba*

Facing page: *a welcoming gallery in Moss Vale, centre of the Southern Highlands*

Canberra and the Australian Capital Territory

Facing page: *Canberra's vast Parliament House, opened in 1988, is topped by an 81m-high flagpole*

Created out of New South Wales farmland after its site was designated in 1908, Canberra is a planned city unlike anywhere else in the nation. Designed by American architect Walter Burley Griffin, and surrounded by parks and gardens, the national capital is a pleasant environment. Canberra is the home of Australia's Federal government; 40 per cent of the 321,000 population is employed in this area. The city is full of diplomatic missions and government departments, and – appealing for the visitor – national museums and galleries. The central focus is man-made Lake Burley Griffin, a location for cruises, from where roads radiate to suburbs and wild bushland. Beyond the city centre, the surrounding Australian Capital Territory (ACT) offers rugged Namadgi National Park, Tidbinbilla Nature Reserve and 1859 Lanyon Homestead.

What to See in Canberra

AUSTRALIAN NATIONAL BOTANIC GARDENS ✪✪

Containing the world's best collection of Australia's unique flora, these gardens feature more than 600 species of eucalyptus trees, a rockery, the delightful rainforest gully, and a Tasmanian alpine garden. Self-guided arrow trails make it easy to find your way around.

Looming behind the gardens is Black Mountain (779m), capped by the futuristic Telstra Tower. There is a spectacular view of the city and surrounding countryside from this structure's viewing gallery.

- ✉ Clunies Ross Street, Acton
- ☎ (02) 6250 9540
- Daily 9–5 (to 8PM in Jan). Closed 25 Dec
- Bus: 34 to University then 10-minute walk
- Café (£–££)
- Good
- Free and free tours

Below: *the planned city of Canberra is an attractive environment of parks, lakeland and leafy suburbs*

AUSTRALIAN WAR MEMORIAL ✪✪

In a dramatic location at the head of Anzac Parade, this impressive monument and museum commemorates the Australians who served in various wars. Its many thousands of displays include aeroplanes, tanks, guns, military memorabilia and artworks.

Treloar Crescent, Campbell
(02) 6243 4211
Daily 10–5
33 Cafés (£–££)
Very good Free

NATIONAL GALLERY OF AUSTRALIA ✪✪✪

This is the nation's premier gallery, and the ideal place to view good examples of Aboriginal and Australian art. European, Asian and American artworks are also featured, and the gallery hosts excellent travelling exhibitions.

Parkes Place, Parkes
(02) 6240 6502
Daily 10–5. Closed Good Fri, 25 Dec
Very good Free

NATIONAL MUSEUM OF AUSTRALIA ✪✪

Opened in 2001, this modern museum explores the key issues, events and people that have shaped Australia. The themed galleries employ state-of-the-art technology and feature the symbols of the nation, indigenous peoples, and stories of ordinary and famous Australians.

Acton Peninsula
(02) 6208 5000
Daily 9–5
34
Good
Free general entry

PARLIAMENT HOUSE ✪✪✪

Canberra's architectural and political centrepiece was completed in 1988, at a staggering cost of over $1,000 million. It contains the House of Representatives and the Senate, public areas featuring fine artworks and craftsmanship. Guided tours are available, and the view from the roof is superb. Also in this Parliamentary Triangle area stands the more modest 1927 Old Parliament House, now housing the National Portrait Gallery.

Capital Hill
(02) 6277 5399
Daily 9–5 (later when Parliament is sitting). Closed 25 Dec
Café (£–££)
31, 34, 39
Excellent Free
Book for Question Time (02) 6277 4889)

QUESTACON ✪✪✪

Also known as The National Science and Technology Centre, this exciting, modern complex brings the world of science alive. Education and entertainment are combined brilliantly in the 170 or so interactive exhibits.

King Edward Ter, Parkes
(02) 6270 2800
Daily 9–5. Closed 25 Dec
Very good Moderate

Food & Drink

It seems almost inconceivable that in the early 1980s Australian food was bland and very much of the traditional English 'meat and two veg' school of cooking: sweet and sour pork or a prawn cocktail were considered the height of culinary sophistication. All this has changed dramatically, largely due to Asian, Middle Eastern and European immigrants introducing their ingredients and styles of cooking.

A seafood feast at the famous Doyle's on The Beach restaurant in Watsons Bay, Sydney

A World of Food

Australian cuisine is now taking the world by storm – the famous chef Robert Carrier predicted on a visit in 1996 that Australian food was the most exciting available, and that it was about to take over the world. Much of this acclaim is due to the development and refinement of 'Modern Australian' cuisine – a form of cooking that has evolved from the use of excellent fresh produce, the fusion of styles and ingredients (anything from Thai to French in one dish), and stylish presentation.

An important component of Australia's inventive cuisine is the superb quality and variety of local produce, from tropical fruits like mangoes to Tasmania's wonderful cheeses and the freshest herbs. The quality of meat is very high, and the variety of seafood will astonish many northern hemisphere visitors: enormous prawns, oysters, crabs, lobsters and delicious tropical fish such as barramundi.

Australia also offers cuisines from all over the world, with Thai, Japanese and other Asian restaurants being particularly popular. You will find everything from Italian and Greek to Lebanese and African cuisines, and one of the greatest joys in this fine climate is eating alfresco, often with a marvellous sea view.

Wine, Beer and Spirits

Wine has been produced in Australia since the late 1830s, and the country's reds and whites are now deservedly world famous. All of the states have some involvement in the industry, but South Australia's Barossa Valley and Coonawarra region, the Hunter Valley of New South Wales, and the Margaret River area of Western Australia are some of the most famous.

Red varieties include Cabernet Sauvignon, Shiraz, Pinot Noir and Merlot, while Chardonnay, Chablis, Sauvignon Blanc and Verdelho are popular whites. There are many hundreds of different labels to choose from, and the best way to discover what you like is to try as many as possible! Ultimately, it all comes down to taste, but it's hard to go wrong with labels like Wolf Blass, Rosemount Estate, Penfolds, Houghtons and Henschke.

Australian beers are now known throughout the world, and there is a huge range to choose from. In addition to Fosters, Tooheys, VB (Victoria Bitter), Reschs, Cascade, Carlton, Swan and XXXX (Fourex) there are popular regional brands, and aficionados will enjoy specialist beers like Hahn, Coopers, Redback and the curiously named Dogbolter.

Australia is not renowned for its spirits, although reasonably good brandy is produced in South Australia. Sampling Bundaberg rum – universally known as 'Bundy' and a delicious by-product of the sugar industry in Queensland – is a must. This fine spirit comes as both underproof (37 per cent) and overproof (a lethal 57.7 per cent), and is usually topped up with cola.

A wonderful range of fresh produce forms the basis of modern Australian cuisine

A small selection of the fine white wines produced in NSW's Hunter Valley

Queensland

Occupying an enormous chunk of the continent's northeast, Queensland is the second largest state after Western Australia. From the subtropical capital of Brisbane in the far south, this vast tract of land – much of which has a hot, sunny and virtually winterless climate – stretches north to well within the tropics.

Many people come here solely to experience the Great Barrier Reef World Heritage Site, a magnificent natural wonder that lies parallel to the coast's sandy beaches and idyllic islands. But Queensland offers much more. Behind the coastal strip, and the hills of the Great Dividing Range, stretches the inhospitable Outback, while in the far north are lush tropical rainforests and the rugged and sparsely populated Cape York Peninsula, which ends just south of Papua New Guinea.

> *'It is often said that Scandinavians find the achievement of plenty linked with mediocrity … so dull that many of them either take to drink or commit suicide. Australians are more likely to commit smugness.'*
>
> ELSPETH HUXLEY
> *Their Shining Eldorado* (1967)

Brisbane – Australia's third-largest city

The Queensland Maritime Museum is adjacent to Brisbane's exciting South Bank parklands

Brisbane

From its crude beginnings as a penal colony – founded in 1824 as an outpost of New South Wales – and its long-standing reputation as a conservative 'country town', Brisbane has undergone a remarkable metamorphosis in recent years, and has embraced progress with much enthusiasm. With a subtropical climate and relatively small population of over 1.6 million, the city has a slower pace of life than that of southern cities, and Queensland's capital has blossomed into a most attractive metropolis.

Although most visitors do not linger for long in Brisbane before heading south to the Gold Coast or north to the attractions of the coast and Great Barrier Reef, there is plenty to see and do here. The city's riverside location is a very important ingredient of its charm: Brisbane stands on a sweeping bend of the Brisbane River, and taking a leisurely cruise or ferry ride around and beyond the city is a highlight of any visit.

There *are* museums, galleries and a few graceful old buildings here, but sunny Brisbane is a largely modern city, concerned for the most part with relaxing and enjoying the good things in life. The brilliantly designed South Bank parklands, which include a swimming lagoon and sandy beach, and the city's many parks and gardens, are ideal places to indulge in such pursuits, as are the islands and beaches of nearby Moreton Bay. You can also explore the pleasant city centre – particularly the shops and outdoor cafés of Queen Street Mall; the Riverside Centre and its ferry wharves, just off Eagle Street; and the Roma Street Parkland. The best view of Brisbane is from the lookout at the top of nearby Mount Coot-tha.

Facing page: *tall glass-fronted buildings loom over the Brisbane River in Queensland's capital city*

What to See in Brisbane

CITY BOTANIC GARDENS ✪✪

Brisbane's premier gardens are in a delightful riverside setting and provide the ideal spot for a break from sightseeing and the heat. The gardens are open around the clock and you can wander among the palm trees, Bunya pines and rainforest area, or take a guided walk.

- Alice Street
- 07) 3403 0666
- Café (£–££)
- The Loop
- Very good
- Free

MOUNT COOT-THA ✪✪

It's worth making the trip to this peak, 6.5km from the city centre, especially at night, for the wonderful view of Brisbane and its surrounds.

You can visit the **Brisbane Botanic Gardens**, with their tropical and native flora, hiking tracks and Aboriginal trails, as well as the Cosmic Skydome and Planetarium, where a dramatic image of the night sky is projected onto a dome.

Botanic Gardens
- Mount Coot-tha Road, Toowong
- (07) 3403 2535
- Daily 8–5:30
- Café (£); restaurant (££)
- 471 Good
- Gardens free, Skydome moderate

QUEENSLAND CULTURAL CENTRE ✪✪✪

This modern South Bank complex includes two important museums – the Queensland Art Gallery, with its fine collection of Australian, Aboriginal, Asian, Pacific and European art; and the Queensland Museum with some particularly good Aboriginal and natural history displays.

Nearby to the south, the large riverside South Bank, parklands (site of the 1988 World Expo) is Australia's best urban park. There is much to see and do here – dining and shopping, an IMAX theatre and weekend markets. The **Queensland Maritime Museum** is also worth a visit.

- Melbourne & Grey streets, South Brisbane
- Gallery (07) 3840 7303; Museum 3840 7555
- Daily: Gallery Mon–Fri 10–5, Sat–Sun 9–5; Museum 9:30–5
- Good Free

Maritime Museum
- Stanley Street
- (07) 3844 5361
- Daily 9:30–4:30

QUEENSLAND SCIENCENTRE ✪✪

With over 170 hands-on exhibits, this is the state's largest science and technology centre. Even the most non-scientific mind, young or old, will be captivated and special shows and demonstrations are held daily. Due to move to new premises in Melbourne and Grey streets end of 2004.

- Queensland Museum, Melbourne & Grey streets, South Brisbane
- (07) 3840 7555

Tropical Cairns, the tourist capital of North Queensland

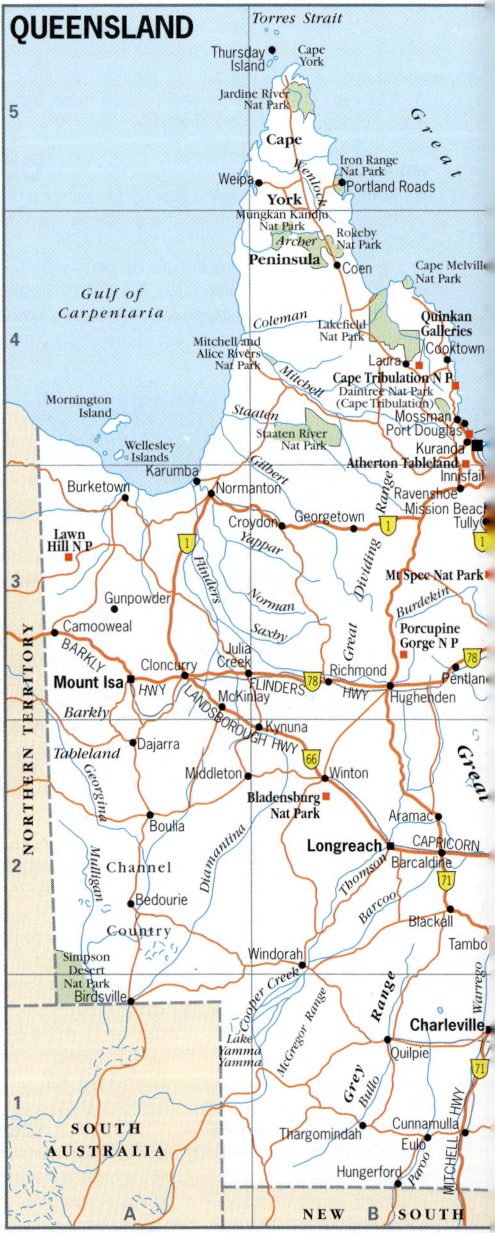

PNG
0
100
200
300
400 km
Marlin Coast
Cairns
Barrier
Reef
Hinchinbrook Island
Ingham
Magnetic Island
Townsville
1234m
Ayr
Charters Towers
Bowen
Prosperine
Conway Nat Park
Whitsunday Islands
Collinsville
Eungella Nat Park
Mackay
Sarina
Moranbah
Denbar Range
Belyendo
BRUCE
HIGHWAY
1
Clermont
Drummond Range
Yeppoon
Great Keppel Island
Emerald
HWY
Alpa
Blackwater
66
Rockhampton
Lake Maraboon
Springsure
Gladstone
Dividing
Range
Moura
Biloela
Carnarvon Nat Park
55
Carnarvon Gorge
Expedition Nat Park
Monto
Range
Bundaberg
Great Sandy Nat Park
Fraser Island
Augathella
HIGHWAY
Dawson
Taroom
Auburn
Childers
Maryborough
Burnett
17
Gympie
Cooloola Nat Park
Sunshine
Coast
Roma
Mitchell
Miles
Kingaroy
Noosa Heads
Nambour
Maranoa
CARNARVON
Condamine
Bunya Mts
Glass House Mountains
Surat
Dalby
Moreton Island
39
Bollon
BRISBANE
Toowoomba
Ipswich
Gold
Coast
St George
Warwick
Surfers Paradise
Dirranbandi
Goondiwindi
Stanthorpe
Lamington Nat Park
Macintyre
WALES
C
D

The lush farmland of the Atherton Tableland contrasts dramatically with the Cairns coastline

What to See in Queensland

ATHERTON TABLELAND (➤ 16, TOP TEN)

www.epa.qld.gov.au
51C2
Carnarvon National Park, via Rolleston
(07) 4984 4505
Daily
Roma, then a drive
Few Free

CARNARVON NATIONAL PARK ✪✪✪

Although it is very remote (over 250km from the nearest town, Roma), a visit to this spectacular park is well rewarded. The Carnarvon Creek has cut through soft sandstone to create 200m cliffs and a 30km-long gorge. There is some good bushwalking, as well as lush vegetation and ancient Aboriginal paintings. Roads may be impassable between January and April.

CAIRNS AND DISTRICT (➤ 16, TOP TEN)

www. charterstowers.qld.gov.au
51C3
Visitor Information Centre, 74 Mosman Street (07) 4752 0314 Daily 9–5. Closed Good Fri, 25–26 Dec, 1 Jan)
Townsville
Townsville

CHARTERS TOWERS ✪✪

Once the second largest city in Queensland, with its own stock exchange, this historic town, situated 135km west of Townsville, was built on gold over a century ago. Today it is a living museum of grand hotels, banks and other National Trust classified buildings. The World Theatre, built in 1891 as an international bank, now serves as a focus for arts and entertainment with a fully restored auditorium, cinema, archival centre and art gallery.

The town has a number of significant events each year, including the Australia Day (26 January) Cricket Festival, the Rodeo (Easter) at nearby Mingela and one of Australia's largest country music festivals on the May Day weekend. (See also Townsville ➤ 54.)

FRASER ISLAND ✪✪✪

At 121km long, this extraordinary World Heritage Site is the world's largest sand island. Yet with extensive rainforest, over 40 freshwater lakes, long sandy beaches, and strangely coloured sand cliffs this is a surprisingly varied environment. The wildlife – including dingoes and wallabies – is prolific, making the island the perfect destination for nature lovers and birdwatchers. Fraser Island is reached by vehicular ferry and a four-wheel-drive vehicle is necessary, unless taking one of the many tours.

www.herveybaytourism.com.au
www.frasercoastholidays.info
51D1
From Hervey Bay
Hervey Bay Tourism Bureau, Maryborough-Hervey Bay roads (☎ (07) 4125 9855
Daily 9–5
None Free
Sunshine Coast (► 54)

GOLD COAST (► 17, TOP TEN)

GREAT BARRIER REEF (► 18–19, TOP TEN)

LAMINGTON NATIONAL PARK ✪✪✪

Temperate and subtropical rainforests, wild mountain scenery with waterfalls, gorges, rock pools, caves and abundant wildlife all combine to make this World Heritage-listed national park a must-see destination for nature lovers. There are 160km of hiking tracks to explore, as well as plenty of easy trails and a rainforest canopy trail. The most accessible and popular sections of the national park are Green Mountains and Binna Burra.

www.epa.qld.gov.au
51D1
Green Mountains (07) 5544 0634; Binna Burra ☎ (07) 5533 3584
Daily
Gold Coast or Brisbane, then a drive
Few Free

World Heritage-listed Fraser Island has long beaches, dunes and unusual sand cliffs

LONGREACH ✪

Longreach in Queensland's Outback was the first home of the national airline Qantas (Queensland and Northern Territory Aerial Services) during the 1920s, and the town has many charming old buildings. The major attraction is the excellent **Australian Stockman's Hall of Fame** and Outback Heritage Centre – a modern complex that pays tribute to the early explorers, pioneers and settlers .

50B2
Australian Stockman's Hall of Fame
Landsborough Highway
(07) 4658 2166
Longreach
Daily 9–5. Closed 25 Dec
Snack bar (£)
Excellent
Expensive

MOUNT TAMBORINE (► 17, TOP TEN)

SUNSHINE COAST ✪✪

Stretching for 65km to the north of Brisbane, the Sunshine Coast region has beautiful white beaches, low-key resorts, and some outstanding national parks. The stylish main resort town of **Noosa Heads** offers sandy beaches and cosmopolitan dining, while nearby attractions include cruising the Noosa River, and exploring the dunes and coloured sand cliffs of Cooloola National Park. Inland, you can tour the Blackall Range region, where there are green hills, charming villages and rich farming country.

www.sunshinecoast.org
51D1
Tourist Information Centre, Hastings Street, Noosa Heads (☎ (07) 5447 4988 Daily 9–5. Closed 25 Dec)
Nambour, then a bus
To Maroochydore
Brisbane (► 48–49), Fraser Island (► 53)

TOWNSVILLE ✪✪

With a population of about 125,000, this historic harbourside settlement is Australia's largest tropical city. The main points of interest are the excellent Reef HQ aquarium complex, the Museum of Tropical Queensland housing relics from the wreck HMS *Pandora*, and the wildlife-rich Billabong Sanctuary. You can visit nearby Magnetic Island, with its fine beaches and abundant wildlife, and take trips to the Great Barrier Reef.

www.townsvilleonline.com.au
51C3
Visitor Centre, Flinders Mall (☎ (07) 4721 3660) Mon–Fri 9–5, Sat–Sun 9–1)
Townsville
Whitsunday Islands

WHITSUNDAY ISLANDS ✪✪✪

Reached via Proserpine and the villages of Airlie Beach and Shute Harbour, these central coast islands form a very popular holiday destination. There are over 70 islands, mostly hilly and forested, with exquisite beaches and incredibly clear turquoise waters. There is a good choice of resorts – from upmarket Hayman to the less sophisticated national park Long Island resort. There are plenty of day trips to the Reef, and the region is perfect for sailing, snorkelling and other water sports.

www.whitsundaytourism.com
51C4
Whitsunday Information Centre, Bruce Highway, Proserpine (Mon–Fri 9–5, Sat–Sun 9–3 ☎ (07) 4945 3711)
Proserpine

The Whitsunday Islands

From Cairns to the Daintree

This extremely scenic drive takes you beyond the holiday city of Cairns via the coastline to charming Port Douglas and the Daintree's World Heritage-listed rainforest.

From central Cairns, take the Captain Cook Highway north out of town.

Stretching for 30km, the beautiful Marlin Coast has many sandy beaches and small resort villages like Trinity Beach and Palm Cove. Other attractions along the way include Cairns Tropical Zoo and Hartley's Crocodile Adventures at Palm Cove, and the Rainforest Habitat near Port Douglas.

Continue on the Highway, then take the Port Douglas turn-off.

Once a sleepy fishing settlement, charming Port Douglas is now a rather exclusive resort village, with upmarket accommodation, dining and shopping, a picturesque harbour and a perfect, long sandy beach.

Return to the Highway and continue to Mossman.

Mossman has a sugar mill and a few other attractions, but this small town is essentially the gateway to the magnificent Daintree rainforest.

Take the Mossman Gorge road.

The significance of this lush region – the province of tropical rainforest, many orchid species, the large, flightless cassowary, enormous birdwing butterflies and a rare tree kangaroo – was recognised in 1988, when the Daintree National Park was World Heritage listed. The most easily accessible part of the Daintree is Mossman Gorge, with its easy 2.7km circuit hiking trail. Cross the Daintree River on the car ferry and you can take the bitumen road as far as Cape Tribulation (50km). There are several places off this road where you can experience coastal tropical rainforests and white-sand beaches.

Return to Cairns via the same route.

Distance
320km

Time
A full day

Start/end point
Central Cairns
50B4

Lunch
On the Inlet (££)
3 Inlet Street, Port Douglas
(07) 4099 5255

Some of Australia's finest tropical rainforest can be found around Cairns, in the verdant Daintree and Wooroonooran national parks

Victoria & Tasmania

Australia's most southerly states hold many surprises – a cooler climate (including winter snows) than many would expect, tranquil farmland, rugged peaks, and coastlines lashed by the wild waters of Bass Strait, which divides Victoria from Tasmania.

Victoria, separated from New South Wales by the country's longest river, the Murray, is small and densely populated by Australian standards. From the gracious capital, Melbourne, it is easy to reach attractions that vary from dramatic coastlines to the ski fields and peaks of the Great Dividing Range.

The compact island state of Tasmania is packed with interest. Its violent convict past intrigues history lovers, while the superb coastal, mountain and wilderness scenery provides endless opportunities for outdoor activities. You can fly to Hobart and Launceston from the mainland, or take the *Spirit of Tasmania* ferry from Melbourne or Sydney to Devonport.

'... a dizzying cocktail of youth, vigour, food and vibrant multiculturalism. Melbournians can turn their dexterous hands to anything.'

WALLPAPER MAGAZINE
(January 1999)

Melbourne's modern Rialto Towers building looms over a 19th-century survivor

The Arts Centre is capped by its distinctive 115m-high spire, a well-known Melbourne landmark

Melbourne

Australia's second largest city, with a population of around 3.5 million, Melbourne is very different from its glossy northern sister. Founded long after Sydney, in 1835, this more elegant, European-style city retains many grand buildings and while its citizens are regarded as more conservative than Sydneysiders, this is not borne out in any tangible way. The climate is often 'four seasons in a day' and can be very hot in summer. Melbourne's cooler winter temperatures are often accompanied by romantic, grey days.

Melbourne has plenty to entertain the visitor. There are over 4,000 restaurants and the dining scene is superb; the shopping rivals that of Sydney; sport is practically a religion; and there is plenty of nightlife – including high-quality theatrical and cultural events at the Victorian Arts Centre and other venues.

A vibrant, sophisticated and dynamic city, bisected by the Yarra River (on which you can take a scenic cruise), the central city area contains many museums and galleries, gracious avenues such as Collins and Spring Streets, and an abundance of green open spaces. Another Melbourne delight is riding the extensive tram network; trams have practically disappeared from all other Australian cities, but in Melbourne this is very much the way to get around.

Melbourne is a city of many ethnic groups – as a visit to Chinatown, with its exotic shops and restaurants and the Museum of Chinese Australian History, or the suburbs of Italian-influenced Carlton and multicultural Richmond reveal. Other enclaves are St Kilda (➤ 60) and South Yarra, with boutiques and the grand 1840s house, Como.

What to See in Melbourne

MELBOURNE CRICKET GROUND ✪✪✪

Visiting this most hallowed of Australia's sporting venues is a must. The city's famous cricket ground, known as the MCG, was the site of the first Australia-England test match in 1877 and the main stadium for the 1956 Olympic Games. Today, the 100,000-capacity ground is used for both cricket and Australian Rules Football, and contains the excellent Olympic and Australian Cricket Hall of Fame.

Yarra Park, Jolimont
(03) 9657 8864
Daily 9:30–4:30. Closed Good Fri, 25 Dec
Coffee shop (£)
Trams 48, 75
Good Moderate
Regular guided tours 10–3 on non event days

MELBOURNE MUSEUM ✪✪

This modern complex is the largest museum in the southern hemisphere. Highlights include the Science and Life Gallery, the Bunjilaka Aboriginal Centre, a 'living forest' complete with wildlife, and an IMAX theatre.

Carlton Gardens, Rathdowne Street
13 1102
Trams 86, 96, City Circle
Excellent Moderate

MELBOURNE OBSERVATION DECK ✪✪

The view from this observation deck, on Level 55 of the tallest building in Melbourne, is simply awe-inspiring. The panorama takes in the city and Port Phillip Bay and stretches as far away as the Dandenong Ranges, about 40km from Melbourne.

525 Collins Street
(03) 9629 8222
Daily 10AM–9PM
Licensed café (££)
City Circle tram
Excellent Moderate

NATIONAL GALLERY OF VICTORIA ✪

Victoria's premier art gallery displays some of the finest artwork in Australia. The international collection, featuring European Old Masters, photography and Asian, pre-Columbian and contemporary art, is housed at the revamped **NGV International** on St Kilda Road, while the new Ian Potter Centre: NGV Australia, at Federation Square, contains Australian art, including Aboriginal, Colonial and contemporary works.

NGV International
180 St Kilda Road
(03) 8620 2222
Daily 10–5. Closed Good Fri, 25 Dec
City Circle tram, 6, 8, 72
Excellent
Free general admission

OLD MELBOURNE GAOL ✪✪

Although rather grim, this mid-19th century building is nonetheless fascinating. The gaol – the scene of 135 hangings, including that of the notorious bushranger Ned Kelly on 11 November 1880 – provides an idea of what colonial 19th-century prison life was like, and contains many intriguing exhibits, including death masks and a flogging triangle.

Russell Street
(03) 9663 7228
Daily 9:30–5. Closed Good Fri, 25 Dec and Anzac Day AM
City Circle tram
Few
Moderate
Queen Victoria Market (➤ 108)
Atmospheric evening tours available

The breathtaking view from the Melbourne Observation Deck, east along Yarra River

www.visitvictoria.com
Any St Kilda tram
Melbourne Visitor Information Centre, Federation Square
(03) 9658 9658
Daily 9–6)

Right: *the beaches of Port Phillip Bay are ideal for relaxation*

ST KILDA ✪✪✪

Melbourne has many lively suburbs which provide a venue for Melburnians to let their hair down. Located on the shores of Port Phillip Bay, St Kilda has been the city's seaside resort since the 1880s, when the pier was constructed. Its waterfront pathway is popular with walkers, cyclists and in-line skaters, and the Luna Park funfair, built in 1912, continues to be a great attraction. There are dozens of bustling cafés and restaurants, particularly on Acland Street. The Sunday arts and crafts markets are good, and you can take a cruise on the bay from the St Kilda Pier.

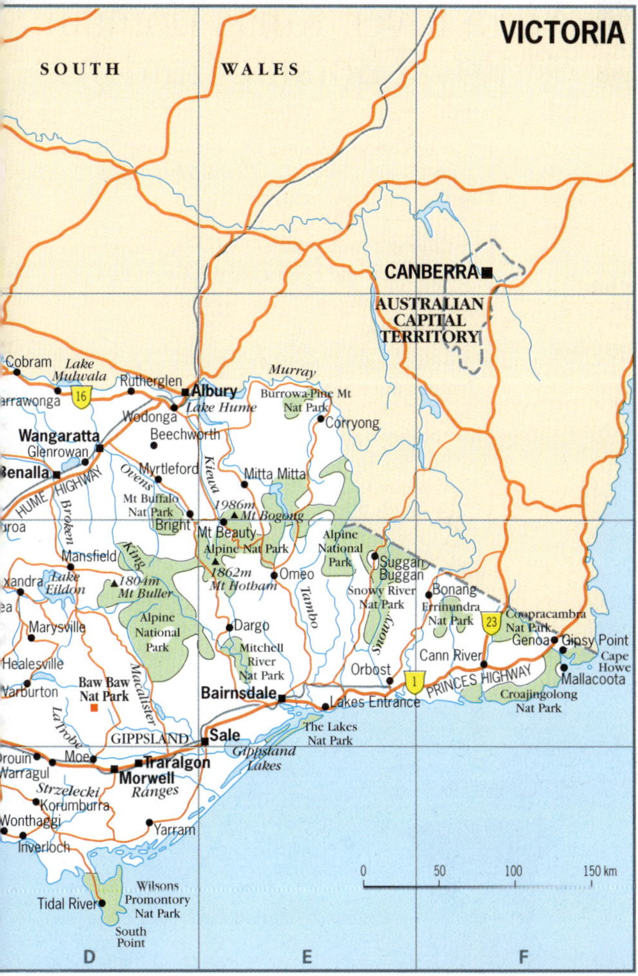
VICTORIA
SOUTH
WALES
CANBERRA
AUSTRALIAN CAPITAL TERRITORY
Cobram
Lake Mulwala
Rutherglen
Albury
Lake Hume
Murray
Burrowa-Pine Mt Nat Park
Corryong
Wodonga
Beechworth
Wangaratta
Glenrowan
Benalla
HUME HIGHWAY
Ovens
Myrtleford
Kiewa
Mitta Mitta
Mt Buffalo Nat Park
Bright
1986m
Mt Bogong
Mt Beauty
Alpine Nat Park
Alpine National Park
Broken
Mansfield
King
1862m
Mt Hotham
Omeo
Suggan Buggan
Lake Eildon
1804m
Mt Buller
Tambo
Snowy River Nat Park
Bonang
Errinundra Nat Park
Coopracambra Nat Park
Genoa
Gipsy Point
Marysville
Alpine National Park
Dargo
Snowy
Cann River
Cape Howe
Mallacoota
Healesville
Macalister
Mitchell River Nat Park
Orbost
PRINCES HIGHWAY
Baw Baw Nat Park
Bairnsdale
Lakes Entrance
Croajingolong Nat Park
La Trobe
The Lakes Nat Park
GIPPSLAND
Sale
Moe
Traralgon
Gippsland Lakes
Warragul
Morwell
Strzelecki Ranges
Korumburra
Wonthaggi
Yarram
Inverloch
0
50
100
150 km
Wilsons Promontory Nat Park
Tidal River
South Point
D
E
F

Yarra River, Kings Domain & Royal Botanic Gardens

Distance
4 km

Time
2–4 hours, including time for a light lunch

Start/end point
Flinders Street Station
60C2
City Circle tram

Lunch
Observatory Cafe (£–££)
Royal Botanic Gardens
(03) 9650 5600

This walk ventures out beyond Melbourne's city centre – along the Yarra River and into the large area of lovely parkland that lies to the south.

Start at Flinders Street Station (corner of Swanston and Flinders Streets), then cross Princes Bridge and turn right for Southbank Promenade.

There are many temptations here in the large Southgate shopping and eating complex. If you can, just admire the view of the city and river from the promenade and continue walking.

Walk under Princes Bridge and follow the path beside the river.

After walking along the Yarra, where you are likely to see many rowing craft, head away from the water at Swan Street Bridge and into the Kings Domain. This lush parkland encompasses impressive Government House, the official residence of the Governor of Victoria.

Facing page: *Ballarat's Sovereign Hill historical park faithfully recreates the old goldrush days*

Continue into the gardens.

The delightful landscaped Royal Botanic Gardens are centred around an extensive ornamental lake. They contain some 60,000 plant species and are one of central Melbourne's most attractive features.

Follow the signs to La Trobe's Cottage.

La Trobe's Cottage, a modest mid-19th-century dwelling, was the home of Charles La Trobe, the state's first governor from 1851 to 1854. It provides a marked contrast to the massive nearby Shrine of Remembrance which contains Victoria's most important war memorial.

From here you can either cross St Kilda Road and take a tram to Flinders Street Station, or walk back via the Kings Domain and call in at the National Gallery of Victoria (► 59).

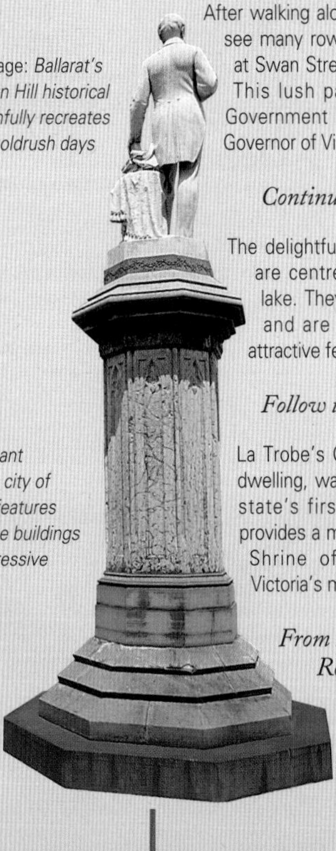

The elegant Victorian city of Ballarat features many fine buildings and impressive statues

What to See in Victoria

BALLARAT

Gold was discovered near Ballarat in 1851, an event that was to bring incredible wealth to the colony, and this elegant city still contains many grand buildings from those days. The main attraction is the excellent **Sovereign Hill** historical park, a re-creation of gold rush era. Other sights are the Ballarat Wildlife Park and Ballarat Fine Art Gallery.

60C2
Sovereign Hill
Bradshaw Street
(03) 5337 1100
Daily 10–5. Closed 25 Dec
Good Expensive

DANDENONG RANGES

Just 40km east of Melbourne are the delightful Dandenong Ranges – cool, moist hills cloaked with eucalypts and rainforest. Their many attractions include Puffing Billy, a quaint steam train which runs between Belgrave and Gembrook, and the William Ricketts Sanctuary, an unusual park featuring Aboriginal-themed sculptures.

www.yarrarangestourism.com
60C2
Upper Ferntree Gully or Belgrave
Visitor Centre, 1211 Burwood Highway, Upper Ferntree Gully ((03) 9758 7522 Daily 9–5. Closed Good Fri, 25 Dec)

GREAT OCEAN ROAD (► 20, TOP TEN)

PHILLIP ISLAND

This scenic island, linked by bridge to the mainland, is famous for its nightly Penguin Parade – tiny fairy penguins waddling ashore to their burrows. The site of the parade and its visitor centre at Summerland Beach are part of the **Phillip Island Nature Park**, which incorporates the island's Koala Conservation Centre (near the main town of Cowes), the ideal place to meet these cuddly marsupials.

www.penguins.org.au
60C1
Phillip Island Nature Park
(03) 5951 2800
Koala Centre daily 10–5:30; Penguins Centre daily from 10AM
From Melbourne
Excellent Moderate

WILSONS PROMONTORY NATIONAL PARK

The spectacular 'Prom' forms the Australian mainland's most southerly point. This is one of Victoria's most popular national parks, offering beaches and superb coastal scenery, rainforests, well-marked hiking tracks, and a wide range of flora and fauna.

www.parkweb.vic.gov.au
61D1
Few Inexpensive
Visitor Centre, Tidal River ((03) 5680 9555 Daily from 8:30)

This reconstructed 1820s watermill is a central feature of Launceston's Penny Royal World entertainment complex

Hobart

Tasmania's capital is one of Australia's most pleasant settlements. The small city of Hobart, on the River Derwent, is full of old colonial buildings; walking is the best way to appreciate the historic atmosphere. While here, you should take a river cruise and a trip to Mount Wellington (1,270m), which dominates the city – the view is sensational.

Left: *The attractive city of Hobart is dominated by the vast bulk of 1,270m-high Mount Wellington*

Tasmania, Australia's most 'English' state, is full of charming old buildings

What to See in Hobart

BATTERY POINT ✪✪✪

With its charming mid-19th-century cottages and houses, craft and antiques shops and quaint streets like Arthur's Circus, this inner city 'village' is Hobart's showpiece. Highlights are the **Narryna Heritage Museum** and the 1818 Signal Station and military base from which the suburb takes its name.

Narryna Heritage Museum
- 103 Hampden Road
- (03) 6234 2791
- Mon–Fri 10:30–5, Sat–Sun 2–5. Closed Good Fri, Anzac Day, 25 Dec
- Few · Inexpensive

ROYAL TASMANIAN BOTANICAL GARDENS ✪✪

These gardens, set high overlooking the river and full of native and exotic plants, form part of the large area of parkland known as the Queens Domain. They include a Conservatory, a Tropical Glasshouse and a museum of botany and horticulture.

- Queens Domain
- (03) 6234 6299
- Daily from 8
- Restaurant (££)
- Good
- Free general admission

SALAMANCA PLACE ✪✪✪

This delightful old dockside street is lined with sandstone warehouses converted into restaurants and arts and crafts shops, and is the venue for Hobart's lively Saturday market (► 108). Antarctic Adventure, in neighbouring Salamanca Square, is well worth a visit, and nearby Sullivans Cove is where the first settlers landed in 1804.

- Salamanca Place
- Markets: Sat 8:30–3
- Many cafés and restaurants (£–£££)
- Few
- Free

TASMANIAN MUSEUM AND ART GALLERY ✪✪✪

Hobart's Tasmanian Museum contains some fine and varied exhibits, particularly on Australian mammals, convict history and Tasmanian Aborigines. The attached art gallery holds a good collection of colonial art. This is an ideal place to start discovering the history of the island.

- 40 Macquarie Street
- (03) 6211 4177
- Daily 10–5. Closed Good Fri, 25 Dec and Anzac Day
- Excellent · Free

What to See in Tasmania

FREYCINET PENINSULA ✪✪✪

Tasmania's east coast is renowned for beautiful scenery, none of which surpasses that of **Freycinet National Park** with its sandy white beaches, granite peaks and abundance of flora, birds and animals. The park is reached via the fishing settlement of Coles Bay, and the town of Bicheno has yet more excellent beaches, great diving, the Sealife Centre and a wildlife park.

www.dpiwe.tas.gov.au
- 65D2
- Visitor Centre, Freycinet Drive, Freycinet NP (☎ (03) 6256 7000 Daily 8–6 (winter 8–5)
- Tassie Link to Bicheno or Coles Bay

LAUNCESTON ✪✪

Tasmania's second city, sited on the Tamar River and founded in 1805 (a year after Hobart), has retained many of its old buildings, which can be viewed on a self-guided walk around town. There are pleasant parks and reserves – a visit to the spectacular Cataract Gorge Reserve is recommended. The Queen Victoria Museum and Art Gallery, located at two sites (city centre and across the river at Inveresk) is also worth a visit. The Launceston region is rich in historic houses and wineries.

www.discovertasmania.com.au
- 65C3
- Information Centre, Cornwall Square, 12–16 St John Street (☎ (03) 6336 3133) Mon–Fri 9–5, Sat 9–3, Sun 9–12)
- Launceston

THE MIDLANDS ✪

The Midlands Highway, running for 200km between Hobart and Launceston, passes through charming and historic towns. Oatlands is full of atmospheric old buildings such as the Court House, while, further north, picturesque Ross is famous for its 1836 bridge and contains the **Tasmanian Wool Centre**, devoted to the state's extensive wool industry.

65C2
Tasmanian Wool Centre
Church Street, Ross
(03) 6381 5466
Daily, generally 9–5
Tasmanian Redline from Hobart
Good Inexpensive

PORT ARTHUR AND THE TASMAN PENINSULA ✪✪✪

Established as a far-flung penal settlement for the worst convict offenders in 1830, Port Arthur has over 30 ruins and historic sites, an excellent museum, and the settlement's poignant burial ground, the Isle of the Dead.

The surrounding Tasman Peninsula has magnificent scenery on the east coast, the Tasmanian Devil Park with an excellent wildlife collection, and the scenic Bush Mill Steam Railway.

www.portarthur.org.au
65D2
Port Arthur Historic Site
(03) 6251 2310
Daily 8:30–dusk
Tassie Link from Hobart
Excellent
Expensive; includes cruise and guided walk

STRAHAN ✪✪

The lightly populated west coast is a region of wild coastline, rivers and forest lands. From the waterside village of Strahan (pronounced 'Strawn') you can go fishing, take a scenic flight, and cruise Macquarie Harbour – once the site of the brutal Sarah Island penal settlement – and the pristine Gordon River, part of the World Heritage-listed Franklin-Gordon Wild Rivers National Park. In town, the **Strahan Visitor Centre** provides a fascinating lesson in local history.

TASMANIA'S WORLD HERITAGE AREA (➤ 25, TOP TEN)

64B2
Strahan Visitor Centre
The Esplanade
(03) 6471 7622
Daily 10–6
Tassie Link to Strahan
Good
Inexpensive

Hobart is delightfully set on the River Derwent

In the Know

If your time in Australia is limited, or you would like to get a real flavour of the country, here are some ideas:

10 Ways To Be A Local

Change your accent – to sound like a real Aussie, draw out the vowels, so that, for example, 'park' becomes 'pahk'.
Relax, Australia is not the place to go in for excessive formality, and 'no worries' is not a popular expression for nothing.
Use 'g'day' instead of 'hello', and call virtually everyone 'mate'.
Wear a hat, not just for fashion, but as a necessity to avoid the sun's harmful rays.
Head for an Aussie pub or two to sample the excellent local beers and wines.
Learn the basic facts about convict, colonial and Aboriginal history, and remember that racist jokes are in extremely bad taste.
Spend most of your time outdoors, particularly on the beach or bushwalking.
Dress casually – summer shorts and sandals are acceptable in nearly all places.
Go to a cricket match, or an Aussie Rules football game in winter, to soak up the atmosphere of the national sports.
Get invited to an Aussie barbecue, where you will enjoy a relaxed meal and a unique cultural experience.

The Melbourne Cricket Ground holds 100,000 spectators

10 Good Places To Have Lunch

Arintji (££) ✉ Federation Square, Melbourne ☎ (03) 9663 9900. An excellent café in the heart of the lively Federation Square precinct.
City Gardens Café (£–££) ✉ City Botanic Gardens, Brisbane ☎ (07) 3229 1554. Good lunchtime fare in a delightful location.
Doyle's on the Beach (££) ✉ 11 Marine Parade, Watsons Bay, Sydney ☎ (02) 9337 2007. Fine seafood with wonderful harbour views.
Fraser's (££) ✉ Fraser Avenue, Kings Park, Perth ☎ (08) 9481 7100. Modern Australian dining in Perth's parklands.
Jolleys Boathouse (££) ✉ Jolleys Lane, Adelaide ☎ (08) 8223 2891. Modern Australian food in a delightful setting.
Juniperberry (££) ✉ National Gallery of Australia, Parkes, Canberra ☎ (02) 6240 6666. Fine Modern Australian cuisine is served in the gallery's sculpture garden.
Mures Upper Deck (££) ✉ Mures Fish Centre, Victoria Dock, Hobart ☎ (03) 6231 1999. A great seafood menu in the perfect waterfront spot.
Nudel Bar (£) ✉ 76 Bourke Street, Melbourne ☎ (03) 9662 9100. Enjoy noodle and pasta dishes from all over the world.
Pee Wee's at the Point (££–£££) ✉ Alec Fong Lim Drive, East Point, Darwin ☎ (08) 8981 6868. On the Darwin beachfront,specialising in Modern Australian cuisine.
Sydney Fish Market (£–£££) ✉ Bank Street, Pyrmont, Sydney ☎ (02) 9660 1611. A wide range of seafood styles and venues.

10 Top Activities

Boating: sail a yacht around Queensland's Whitsunday Islands, or rent a houseboat on the Murray River.
Bushwalking: there are countless places to go hiking, but try Tasmania and the Blue Mountains near Sydney.
Cross-country skiing: the conditions are ideal around the ski fields of Victoria, Tasmania and New South Wales (Jun–Oct).
Fishing: from trout fishing in Tasmania's lakes to big-game marlin wrestling off Cairns.
Four-wheel-driving adventures: the Pinnacles in WA is an ideal venue.
Golf: in Australia golf is a sport for everyone. There are excellent courses everywhere, but those on the Gold Coast are particularly recommended.
Horse riding: the south-east is ideal – around the Snowy Mountains of NSW and Victoria's alpine areas.
Scuba diving and snorkelling: there is nowhere better than along the Great Barrier Reef.
Surfing: the quintessential Aussie sport – Sydney's coastline, Bells Beach in Victoria and Margaret River in the west are all good spots.
Tennis: you will find day/night courts in every major city.

5 Great Views

- From the Sydney Tower, Sydney.
- Brisbane – from Mount Coot-tha.
- From Mount Wellington, Hobart.
- From Melbourne Observation Deck, Melbourne.
- From Telstra Tower on Black Mountain, Canberra.

5 Exceptional Lesser Known Destinations

- Bathurst and Melville islands, Northern Territory: the home of the indigenous Tiwi people and their traditional culture.
- Coober Pedy, South Australia: an opal mining town with most buildings underground.
- Jervis Bay, New South Wales: white sands, clear blue waters and unspoilt bushland.
- Ningaloo Reef, near Exmouth, Western Australia: the diving here rivals that of the Great Barrier Reef.
- Norfolk Island: an external territory of Australia, packed with fascinating convict and colonial history.

Boating is very popular around the long coastline

South Australia & Northern Territory

Founded in 1836 and settled by non-convicts, South Australia has an extraordinary range of scenery. There are fertile farming lands in the south, but the vast majority of the land is taken up by the arid deserts and peaks of the Outback. The state is vast, and has many attractions other than those included here, such as the remote opal mining town of Coober Pedy.

The sparsely populated Northern Territory is still real frontier country. Almost half of the population, a large proportion of which are Aboriginal people, lives in cosmopolitan Darwin. From the tropical 'Top End' to the desert lands of the 'Red Centre' around Alice Springs, now connected by the famous Ghan train the Northern Territory is endlessly fascinating, with superb natural attractions like Kakadu and Uluru (Ayers Rock).

'It's so empty and featureless, like a newspaper that has been entirely censored. We used to drive for miles, always expecting that around the next corner there'd be something to look at, but there never was. That is the charm of Australia.'

ROBERT MORLEY
on Australia's Outback (1949)

Waterfall, Kakadu National Park

Adelaide

South Australia's capital was first settled in December 1836, when HMS *Buffalo* docked at Glenelg with her 'cargo' of free settlers. Unlike many Australian cities, Adelaide was planned – Englishman Colonel William Light was responsible for the grid of city-centre streets. Adelaide was once known as the 'City of Churches' and for its staid, conservative citizens, but today the 1.1 million population enjoys an enviable lifestyle and a Mediterranean climate.

A street in Adelaide – the capital of South Australia and one of the nation's most pleasant cities

Surrounded by large areas of parkland, and with the Adelaide Hills forming a splendid backdrop, Adelaide's compact and mostly flat city centre is a delightful place to explore; there are many old buildings, relatively little traffic, and a sense of calm which is rare in urban environments. This elegant city is famous for its café and restaurant scene, as well as for a thriving artistic and cultural life. The ideal time to be here is during the biennial (every even-numbered year), internationally acclaimed Adelaide Festival of Arts, when the city comes alive with everything from classical music concerts to outrageous fringe theatre.

In addition to visiting the museums and attractions detailed below, you should take a cruise on the placid and scenic River Torrens, which passes through the city. Within the metropolitan area, you can also visit the charming seaside suburb of Glenelg, where the first settlers landed in 1836 – it can be reached by an enjoyable tram ride from the city centre. The historic settlement of Port Adelaide was once the city's harbour town, but now concentrates on its heritage attractions, including the well presented South Australian Maritime Museum (➤ 111) and the National Railway Museum complex, the largest of its kind in the country.

What to See in Adelaide

ART GALLERY OF SOUTH AUSTRALIA AND NORTH TERRACE ✪✪✪

A stroll down North Terrace, Adelaide's grandest avenue, is the best way to see the city's historic buildings, several of which are open to the public. At the western end are the Adelaide Casino in a restored 1920s railway station, Old Parliament House, and the latter's neighbouring, much more impressive successor. East of King William Street lie the South Australian Museum, the Art Gallery of South Australia, and 1840s Ayers House, former home of Sir Henry Ayers, who was seven times Premier of South Australia and the inspiration behind the naming of Ayers Rock.

- Art Gallery of South Australia: North Terrace
- (08) 8207 7000
- Daily 10–5. Closed Good Fri AM, 25 Dec
- Art Gallery Café (£–££)
- City Loop
- Good
- Free general admission
- Free guided tours at regular intervals.

GLENELG ✪✪

Take the vintage tram from Victoria Square in the city to this popular seaside suburb where you can soak up the history and have a relaxed lunch in one of the many excellent eating establishments. Walk the pier and be sure to check out the replica of the HMS *Buffalo*, where there is an interesting museum and a popular family restaurant.

- Glenelg Visitor Centre, Foreshore (☎ (08) 8294 5833 Mon–Fri 9–5, Sat–Sun 10–3)
- Glenelg tram or 342 bus
- Good Free

SOUTH AUSTRALIAN MUSEUM ✪✪✪

In addition to the usual natural history and general ethnographic and anthropological displays, this better-than-average museum has an internationally acclaimed collection of Aboriginal Australian artefacts. Another highlight is the large Pacific Cultures exhibit.

- North Terrace
- (08) 8207 7500
- Daily 10–5. Closed Good Fri, 25 Dec
- City Loop
- Good Free

TANDANYA NATIONAL ABORIGINAL CULTURAL INSTITUTE ✪✪✪

This illuminating Aboriginal centre is one of few of its kind in Australia. Including galleries with high-quality changing art exhibitions, workshops, and an area for dance and other performing arts, Tandanya (the local Aboriginal name for the Adelaide region) is a must for visitors. The centre has a shop selling gifts and a variety of good Aboriginal-made items.

- 253 Grenfell Street
- (08) 8224 3200
- Daily 10–5
- City Loop
- Good
- Inexpensive
- Adelaide Botanic Garden and Adelaide Zoo (➤ 76); Art Gallery of SA/North Terrace (see above)

Shop for high-quality Aboriginal arts and crafts at Adelaide's Tandanya Cultural Institute

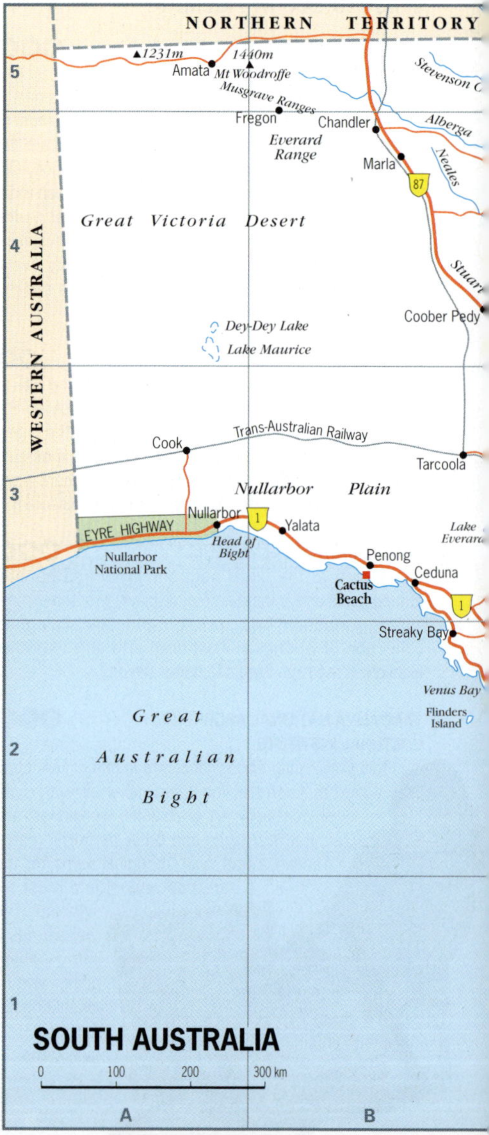
NORTHERN TERRITORY
WESTERN AUSTRALIA
1231m
1440m
Amata
Mt Woodroffe
Musgrave Ranges
Fregon
Chandler
Everard Range
Marla
87
Alberga
Neales
Great Victoria Desert
Coober Pedy
Dey-Dey Lake
Lake Maurice
Cook
Trans-Australian Railway
Tarcoola
Nullarbor Plain
Nullarbor
1
Yalata
EYRE HIGHWAY
Head of Bight
Nullarbor National Park
Penong
Cactus Beach
Ceduna
Streaky Bay
Venus Bay
Flinders Island
Great Australian Bight
SOUTH AUSTRALIA
0
100
200
300 km
A
B
5
4
3
2
1

The Murray River, once the domain of paddle steamers, is now a popular place for houseboating holidays

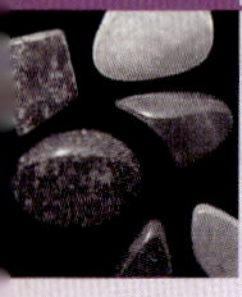

North Adelaide & City Parklands

Distance
2km

Time
2–4 hours, depending on time at the zoo and in the gardens

Start point
Adelaide Festival Centre
75D2
City Loop

End point
North Terrace
75D2
City Loop

Lunch
The Oxford (££)
101 O'Connell Street, North Adelaide
(08) 8267 2652

An easy walk which takes you beyond the city centre and into some of Adelaide's delightful parklands.

Start on King William Road, just beyond the junction with North Terrace.

The Adelaide Festival Centre is the heart of Adelaide's arts scene. The large modern building houses several performance halls and a performing arts museum. River cruises start in front of the centre.

Continue north on King William Road, crossing the River Torrens on Adelaide Bridge.

St Peter's Cathedral dates from 1869; the bells are the heaviest and finest in the southern hemisphere.

Walk along Pennington Terrace to reach Montefiore Hill.

From the look-out, 'Light's Vision', next to the statue of Colonel William Light, there are wonderful views.

Walk up Jeffcott Street towards Wellington Square, then turn right at Archer Street to reach O'Connell Street.

The elegant suburb of North Adelaide contains many grand old homes. A lively pub, café and gallery scene thrives along O'Connell and Melbourne streets.

From O'Connell Street, turn left into Brougham Place, then right into Frome Road to reach Melbourne Street. Return to Frome Road and cross the River Torrens via Albert Bridge to Adelaide's small zoo.

Adelaide Zoo is one of Australia's oldest. It has good aviaries and reptile house and an entertaining collection of Australian mammals.

The plaza of the Adelaide Festival Centre features some unusual, brightly coloured sculptures

Follow the signs to the Botanic Garden.

The Adelaide Botanic Garden is delightful. Don't miss the Bicentennial Conservatory, a vast glass dome containing a tropical rainforest, and the nearby National Wine Centre.

Return to North Terrace.

What to See in South Australia

ADELAIDE HILLS ✪✪

Just 20 minutes east of the city, this region of hills, bushland, vineyards and picturesque small towns is a popular weekend destination. Attractions include good views from the summit of Mount Lofty, botanic gardens, the acclaimed National Motor Museum at Birdwood, and Warrawong Earth Sanctuary – an important wildlife reserve. The German-style main town of Hahndorf has fine artworks in the Hahndorf Academy.

www. visitadelaidehills.com.au
75D2
Visitor Information Centre, 41 Main Street, Hahndorf (☎ (08) 8388 1185 Mon–Fri 9–5, Sat–Sun 10–4)
From Adelaide
Barossa Valley (below)

BAROSSA VALLEY ✪✪✪

The wine-producing area of the Barossa was settled in the 1830s by Silesians and Prussians, and this picturesque valley is characterised by distinctive European architecture, traditions and cuisine. You can visit some of the 50 or so wineries, and enjoy the ambience of towns and villages like Tanunda, Bethany, Lyndoch and Angaston.

www.barossa-region.org
75D2
Barossa Wine and Visitor Information Centre, 66–68 Murray Street, Tanunda (☎ (08) 8563 0600 Mon–Fri 9–5, Sat–Sun 10–4. Closed Good Fri, 25 Dec)
From Adelaide
Adelaide Hills (above)

COOBER PEDY (➤ 69)

COONAWARRA REGION (➤ PANEL BELOW)

FLINDERS RANGES NATIONAL PARK ✪✪

A rugged desert mountain chain containing one of the most ancient landscapes on earth. Plenty of wildlife can be found, while there are several good hikes that allow you to see the diverse plantlife. The highlights of the Park are Wilpena Pound, an enormous 80-sq km elevated amphitheatre surrounded by sheer cliffs, and St Mary's Peak (1,165m), a challenging walk for experienced hikers. The area features abundant Aboriginal art.

www.environment.sa.gov.au
75D3
Wilpena Visitor Centre (☎ (08) 8648 0048 Daily 8–6)
Inexpensive
From Adelaide

KANGAROO ISLAND ✪✪✪

Australia's third largest island is a relaxed place with spectacular scenery, remarkable wildlife, and pleasant small towns like the main settlement of Kingscote. There are rugged cliffs and sandy beaches; a large part of the island is within Flinders Chase National Park, domain of kangaroos, koalas and prolific birdlife; and you can view Australian sea lions from close quarters at Seal Bay Conservation Park.

www.tourkangarooisland.com.au
75C1
Kangaroo Island Gateway Visitor Centre, Howard Drive, Pennesaw (☎ (08) 8553 1185 Mon–Fri 9–5, Sat–Sun 10–4. Closed 25 Dec)
From Adelaide
From Cape Jervis

Did you know ?

Although the Barossa Valley is South Australia's most famous wine area, the Clare Valley further north, the Coonawarra region in the southeast, and McLaren Vale, south of Adelaide, also produce fine wines. Some of the best wineries in these areas are Knappstein Wines at Clare, Penfolds at Coonawarra, and Hardy's McLaren Vale.

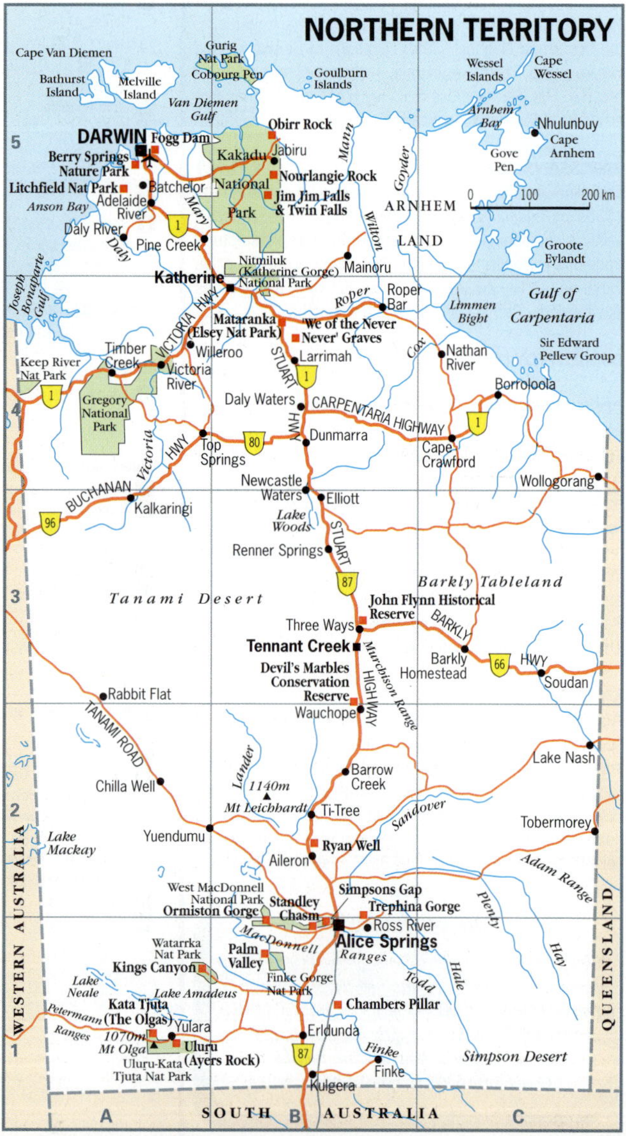
NORTHERN TERRITORY
Cape Van Diemen
Bathurst Island
Melville Island
Gurig Nat Park
Cobourg Pen
Goulburn Islands
Van Diemen Gulf
Wessel Islands
Cape Wessel
Arnhem Bay
Nhulunbuy
Cape Arnhem
Gove Pen
DARWIN
Fogg Dam
Berry Springs Nature Park
Litchfield Nat Park
Batchelor
Anson Bay
Adelaide River
Daly River
Daly
Pine Creek
Mary
Kakadu National Park
Obirr Rock
Jabiru
Nourlangie Rock
Jim Jim Falls & Twin Falls
Mann
Goyder
Wilton
ARNHEM LAND
0 100 200 km
Groote Eylandt
Mainoru
Nitmiluk (Katherine Gorge) National Park
Katherine
Joseph Bonaparte Gulf
Roper
Roper Bar
Limmen Bight
Gulf of Carpentaria
Mataranka (Elsey Nat Park)
'We of the Never Never' Graves
Larrimah
Cox
Nathan River
Sir Edward Pellew Group
Borroloola
Keep River Nat Park
Timber Creek
Victoria River
Willeroo
VICTORIA HWY
STUART HWY
Gregory National Park
Daly Waters
CARPENTARIA HIGHWAY
Dunmarra
Cape Crawford
Top Springs
Victoria HWY
Wollogorang
BUCHANAN
Kalkaringi
Newcastle Waters
Elliott
Lake Woods
Renner Springs
STUART
Barkly Tableland
Tanami Desert
John Flynn Historical Reserve
Three Ways
BARKLY HWY
Tennant Creek
Barkly Homestead
Soudan
Devil's Marbles Conservation Reserve
Murchison Range
HIGHWAY
Rabbit Flat
Wauchope
TANAMI ROAD
Lake Nash
Barrow Creek
Lander
1140m
Mt Leichhardt
Chilla Well
Ti-Tree
Sandover
Tobermorey
Yuendumu
Lake Mackay
Ryan Well
Aileron
Adam Range
West MacDonnell National Park
Ormiston Gorge
Standley Chasm
Simpsons Gap
Trephina Gorge
Ross River
Plenty
Hay
MacDonnell Ranges
Alice Springs
Watarrka Nat Park
Kings Canyon
Palm Valley
Finke Gorge Nat Park
Todd
Hale
Lake Neale
Lake Amadeus
Kata Tjuta (The Olgas)
Petermann Ranges
Chambers Pillar
Yulara
1070m
Mt Olga
Uluru (Ayers Rock)
Uluru-Kata Tjuṯa Nat Park
Erldunda
Finke
Simpson Desert
Kulgera
WESTERN AUSTRALIA
QUEENSLAND
SOUTH AUSTRALIA
A B C
1 2 3 4 5

Mindil Beach is the ideal spot to view Darwin's often spectacular tropical sunsets

Darwin

The Northern Territory's capital and largest city, with a multiracial population of about 108,000, was founded in 1869. Bombed by the Japanese during World War II, Darwin suffered another catastrophe in 1974, when Cyclone Tracy virtually flattened the city. Located on vast Darwin Harbour (on which a cruise is highly recommended), this tropical, modern settlement is a laid-back place. Few reminders of Darwin's history remain, but you can visit the 1883 Fannie Bay Gaol and take a historical walk around the city centre.

DARWIN WHARF PRECINCT

This busy waterfront complex includes shops, cafés and restaurants, and you can go fishing or take a boat excursion from the wharf. The Australian Pearling Exhibition is here, as are the Indo Pacific Marine – an award-winning education and environment centre – and the Deckchair Outdoor Cinema.

Stokes Hill Wharf
(08) 8981 4268
Daily, attractions 10–5
Good
Moderate (for attractions)

GEORGE BROWN DARWIN BOTANIC GARDENS

Containing the southern hemisphere's most extensive collection of tropical palms, an orchid farm, a rainforest area and wetlands flora, Darwin's gardens are a delightful place in which to relax or escape the heat.

Gardens Road, The Gardens
(08) 8981 1958
Daily 7–7
Good Free

MINDIL BEACH

Although swimming is not recommended, due to box jellyfish, sharks and crocodiles, this pleasant beach offers a park, wonderful sunsets, Darwin's casino and the famous Mindil Beach Sunset Markets (► 108).

Mindil Beach Sunset Markets
Apr–Oct Thu 5–10, Sun 4–10

MUSEUM AND ART GALLERY OF THE NORTHERN TERRITORY

This well-planned, modern complex includes the Maritime Museum, a good collection of Aboriginal and Australian art, and displays on local and military history, natural science and Cyclone Tracy. There is a café in the museum.

Conacher St, Bullocky Point
(08) 8999 8201
Mon–Fri 9–5, Sat–Sun 10–5. Closed Good Fri, 25 Dec
Excellent Free

What to See in the Northern Territory

www. centralaustraliantourism.com
78B1
Central Australian Tourism Industry Association, 60 Gregory Terrace ((08) 8952 5800 Mon–Fri 8:30–5:30, Sat–Sun 9–4. Closed Good Fri, 25 Dec)
The Ghan from Darwin, Adelaide and Sydney
Alice Springs

ALICE SPRINGS

Affectionately known as 'The Alice', this unpretentious Outback town at the heart of the continent was founded as a remote Overland Telegraph station in 1871. Alice Springs is full of attractions: you can take a camel ride, or visit the Old Telegraph Station, the Royal Flying Doctor Service base, a variety of museums and the fascinating Aboriginal Art and Culture Centre.

Nearby, the rugged MacDonnell Ranges contain steep gorges, nature reserves, historic settlements and homesteads, ancient Aboriginal sites, national parks, and Palm Valley, where 3,000 rare and ancient palm trees grow.

A veteran aircraft of the renowned Royal Flying Doctor Service

www. tennantcreektourism.com.au
78B3
Tennant Creek Centre, Peko Road ((08) 8962 3388 Generally Mon–Fri 9–5, Sat 9–12)

DEVIL'S MARBLES CONSERVATION RESERVE

Beside the Stuart Highway to the south of Tennant Creek, these huge, curiously eroded granite boulders are significant in Aboriginal mythology – legend says they are the eggs of the Rainbow Serpent.

KAKADU NATIONAL PARK (➤ 21, TOP TEN)

www.krta.com.au
78B4
Katherine Region Tourist Association, Lindsay Street ((08) 8972 2650 Mon–Fri 8:30–5, Sat–Sun 9–2)
The Ghan from Darwin and Alice Springs
Katherine

KATHERINE AND NITMILUK NATIONAL PARK

Katherine, the Territory's third largest settlement, is a pleasant town with a museum, a nature reserve and some historic buildings. The main attraction is nearby Nitmiluk (Katherine Gorge) National Park, containing 13 dramatic sandstone gorges. The best way to appreciate Nitmiluk is by taking a cruise on the Katherine River.

ULURU–KATA TJUTA NATIONAL PARK (➤ 26, TOP TEN)

www.nt.gov.au/ipe/pwcnt
78A1
Central Australia Tourism Industry Association, Alice Springs (above)
None
Few Free

WATARRKA NATIONAL PARK

This remote, rugged desert park, north of Uluru, is famous for Kings Canyon – a spectacular sandstone gorge with walls over 200m high. Visitors can explore lush waterholes, wonder at the strangely weathered rocks of the Lost City, and take a challenging bushwalk. There is a wide variety of flora and fauna, including some extraordinary ancient palm trees.

Darwin to Litchfield National Park

This drive makes an easy day trip, and the itinerary takes in several fun attractions outside Darwin, plus a superb national park.

From Darwin's centre, follow the signs to the Stuart Highway and Winnellie.

In the outer suburb of Winnellie, the Australian Aviation Heritage Centre has a good collection of aircraft, including a massive B-52 bomber.

Continue south on the Highway.

Darwin Crocodile Farm, 40km south of Darwin, has over 8,000 saltwater and freshwater crocodiles. This farm and research centre is the ideal place to inspect the most fearsome of reptiles.

Distance
280km

Time
A full day is necessary

Start/end point
Central Darwin
78A5

Lunch
Territory Wildlife Park (£)
Cox Peninsula Road, Berry Springs
(08) 8988 7200

Continue south, then take the Berry Springs turn-off.

Berry Springs has two major attractions – the large Territory Wildlife Park, with its excellent collection of native fauna, and the nearby Berry Springs Nature Park, a great spot for a swim or a barbecue.

Return to the Stuart Highway and drive south. Take the Batchelor turn-off.

The small settlement of Batchelor, once a dormitory town for workers at the nearby Rum Jungle uranium field, is best known as the gateway to Litchfield National Park.

Continue for another 21km into the park.

Litchfield National Park, a rugged yet delightful reserve, was little known before the mid-1980s, as it was on private land. Nowadays, the many visitors come to enjoy the four spectacular waterfalls, refreshing swimming holes, hiking trails and superb views of the surrounding region. Other highlights are a small 1930s pioneers' homestead; tall 'magnetic' termite mounds, so called because they always face north–south; and the Lost City, an area of curious sandstone pillars.

Return to Darwin via Batchelor and the Stuart Highway.

Spring-fed waterfalls are a highlight of Litchfield National Park, a pleasant drive south of Darwin

Western Australia

Western Australia takes up almost a third of the continent, but is home to just under 2 million people, the vast majority living in Perth and its port, Fremantle. Much of the terrain is arid and used for little more than cattle farming and mining. The discovery of gold in the southeast in the 1890s initially brought prosperity, and modern Western Australia has boomed because of the extraordinary wealth created by iron ore mining in particular.

Natural wonders here are remarkable: tall forests in the southwest; a coastline of white sandy beaches and rugged cliffs; extraordinary wildlife, including marsupials like the numbat and quokka, unique to the state; and the dramatic rock formations of the Kimberley in the far north. Many of the glorious southern wild flowers are also found nowhere else in Australia. Although there is much to see here, remember that distances are vast – flying is the best option for getting around.

'An ingenious but sarcastic Yank, when asked what he thought of WA, declared that it was the best country he had ever seen to run through an hour-glass.'

ANTHONY TROLLOPE
Australia & New Zealand (1873)

The Pinnacles, Nambung National Park

The modern city of Perth provides an enviable lifestyle, centred around its beaches and the delightful Swan River

Perth

Founded in 1829 by free settlers, and initially known as the Swan River Colony, Perth began life as an incredibly isolated outpost of Sydney and the eastern part of the continent. This isolation continues today. Despite its prosperity and cosmopolitan ambience, Perth is the world's most remote city – separated from the east by the desert lands of the Nullarbor Plain, with the nearest large centre, Adelaide, over 2,700km away.

Much of Perth's charm is due to its location. The city is in a delightful setting on the broad Swan River; some of Australia's best urban beaches lie to the west; and the metropolitan area is backed by the low hills of the Darling Range to the east. The climate is warm and sunny, the generally rather affluent lifestyle is enviable, and the atmosphere is very relaxed for a state capital.

Perth's small and mostly modern city centre, much of which was reconstructed during the 1980s with the proceeds of the state's mineral wealth, offers quite a few attractions of its own. There are historic buildings, many parks and gardens, excellent restaurants and some good nightlife venues. But the true delights of this western capital lie a little beyond the city centre. Perth is seen at its best from the white sandy beaches of Cottesloe and Scarborough, and on cruises up the Swan River to the vineyards of the fertile Avon Valley. Another Perth highlight is the ferry trip to the atmospheric port town of Fremantle, just 19km downstream.

What to See in Perth

FREMANTLE ✪✪✪

Perth's seaport is reached by train or a short boat trip down the Swan River. Fremantle's harbourside location, delightful old buildings and quaint streets make it irresistible. Don't miss the informative Western Australian Maritime Museum, the Fremantle Motor Museum, the markets, the Round House and the austere Fremantle Prison.

www.fremantle.com
Fremantle Tourist Bureau, Town Hall, Kings Square (☎ (08) 9431 7878 Mon–Fri 9–5, Sat 10–3)
Fremantle

KINGS PARK ✪✪✪

Overlooking the city and the Swan River, this popular 400-hectare reserve consists largely of unspoilt bushland, with colourful wild flowers and prolific birdlife, although it includes the Western Australian Botanic Garden, and the impressive State War Memorial. The best way to explore is by hiring a bike; or join a free guided walking tour.

Off Fraser Avenue
(08) 9480 3600
Daily
Restaurants (£–££)
33 or Perth Tram bus
Good
Free

ST GEORGE'S TERRACE ✪✪

A walk along Perth's grandest avenue is the ideal way to see some of the city's historic buildings. Near Pier Street you will find the 1850s Deanery, the neo-Gothic St George's Cathedral, and Government House (1864). Closer to Kings Park are the 1850s Old Perth Boys' School, now owned by the National Trust and also containing a gift shop and café, and the Cloisters, a former collegiate school.

St George's Terrace
Some buildings open weekdays 9–5.
Central Area Transit bus
Good
Free
Kings Park (see above), Western Australian Museum (see below)

An old well at Fremantle's historic Round House

WESTERN AUSTRALIAN MUSEUM ✪✪✪

Incorporating Perth's original 1850s gaol and an early settler's cottage, this is the state's largest and most comprehensive museum. There are displays on Western Australian mammals, birds and marine life, but the highlight is the Aboriginal gallery. While in this northern city area, visit the Art Gallery of Western Australia, on nearby James Street.

James Street Mall
(08) 9427 2700
Daily 9:30–5. Closed Good Fri, 25 Dec, 1 Jan
Coffee shop (£)
Central Area Transit bus
Good
Donation (moderate for special exhibitions)
St George's Terrace

Did you know ?

Western Australia's capital was originally called the Swan River Colony, after the river which flows through the city. The river itself was named for the black swans which impressed and astonished the 17th-century explorer Willem de Vlamingh and many early settlers. These unusual birds are still common around Perth today.

The lilac blossom of a Jacaranda tree, Perth

Rugged sandstone gorges are a striking feature of Western Australia's landscape

Aptly named Wave Rock

What to See in Western Australia

www.albanytourist.com.au
86B1
Albany Visitor Centre, Old Railway Station, Proudlove Parade (08) 9841 1088 Daily 9–5)
Albany
Pemberton (➤ 89)

ALBANY ✪✪

Now a scenic holiday resort, Albany was Western Australia's first settlement. Founded three years before Perth, the town developed into a port and whaling centre – the old whaling station is now the fascinating Whale World museum, and there is whale watching here from August to October. This attractive town contains the 1850s Residency and Old Gaol, both now museums. The coastline and beaches are spectacular, and you should also visit the rugged mountain country of Stirling Range National Park, which lies 100km inland.

www.kalgoorlie.com
87C2
Kalgoorlie Goldfields Visitor Centre, 250 Hannan Street, Kalgoorlie (08) 9021 1966 Mon–Fri 8:30–5, Sat–Sun 9–5. Closed 25 Dec)
Kalgoorlie
Prospector from Perth

KALGOORLIE-BOULDER ✪✪

Prospectors flocked to this barren Outback region, 600km east of Perth, when rich gold deposits were discovered near Kalgoorlie in 1893. The area still produces nickel and gold. The city of Kalgoorlie and its smaller neighbour, Boulder, contain fine old buildings, the Australian Prospectors and Miners Hall of Fame, at the Hannans North Mine complex, and a Royal Flying Doctor base. The well-preserved ghost town of Coolgardie is also worth a visit.

THE KIMBERLEY (➤ 22, TOP TEN)

www.margaretriver.com
86A1
Margaret River Tourist Bureau, Tunbridge Road/Bussell Highway (08) 9757 2911) Daily 9–5)

MARGARET RIVER ✪✪✪

Some of Australia's best wines are produced around this picturesque town, 280km south of Perth, in over 50 wineries, including the excellent Vasse Felix and Leeuwin Estate. You can sample the produce at many of them. The area has wonderful beaches, great surfing and bush-walking along the cliffs of nearby Leeuwin-Naturaliste

National Park. The Margaret River township has galleries, crafts shops and fine restaurants.

The Australind to Bunbury, then a bus

NAMBUNG NATIONAL PARK AND THE PINNACLES ✪✪✪

This coastal national park to the north of Perth bristles with thousands of limestone pillars and needles reaching up to 6m in height. Early Dutch seafarers believed they had sighted a ruined city, but the Pinnacles are actually the fossils of ancient plants. The area has good beaches.

www.calm.wa.gov.au
86B2
Nambung National Park, via Cervantes
(08) 9652 7043
Daily
None
Few
Inexpensive

PEMBERTON ✪✪

A visit to the small town of Pemberton, at the heart of the southwest's 'Tall Timber Country', reveals a very different aspect of Western Australia. Giant 400-year-old hardwood trees – jarrah, karri and marri – tower 100m above the dense undergrowth. Ride the Pemberton Tramway through the forests and visit the local sawmill and a museum.

www.pembertontourist.com.au
86B1
Pemberton Visitor Centre, Brockman Street ((08) 9776 1133 Daily 9–5. Closed 25 Dec);
The Australind to Bunbury, then a bus

ROTTNEST ISLAND ✪✪✪

This idyllic island lies just 90 minutes by ferry or 15 minutes by air from Perth. First discovered by Dutch seafarers in the 17th century and mistakenly named 'rat's nest' for the quokkas (small marsupials that still roam the island), Rottnest has almost 40km of extraordinarily white beaches, crystal-clear waters that are perfect for fishing, diving and snorkelling, and a relaxed, car-free atmosphere.

www.rottnest.wa.gov.au
86B1
Rottnest Island Visitor Centre, Thomson Bay ((08) 9372 9752 Daily 8:30–5)
Inexpensive (includes ferry)
Rottnest Island

SHARK BAY ✪✪

With its islands and 1,500km of indented coastline, the World Heritage Site of Shark Bay, on the state's mid-north coast, is a marine wonderland. This vast inlet is famous for the Monkey Mia beach, where wild dolphins come close to the shore to be hand fed. Visit dazzlingly white Shell Beach and François Peron National Park, and see Hamelin Pool's stromatolites, some of the world's oldest living organisms.

www.sharkbay.asn.au
www.calm.wa.gov.au
86A3
SB Tourist Bureau, 71 Knight Terrace, Denham ((08) 9948 1253 Daily 9–5)
Inexpensive Denham

WAVE ROCK ✪✪

This stunning rock formation is one of Western Australia's strangest natural wonders. Wave Rock is a 14m-high granite wall, more than 100m long, which has been eroded over almost 3,000 million years into the shape of a breaking wave. Other curious (and curiously named) formations in the area include the Breakers and the Hippo's Yawn, and you can also look at Aboriginal hand paintings at Mulkas Cave.

www.heartlands.com.au
87C1
Hyden Tourist Centre, Wave Rock ((08) 9880 5182 Daily 9–5 or 6)
None
Few Free

South of Perth

Distance
360km

Time
A full day or more

Start/end point
Central Perth
✚ 86B1

Lunch
Benesse Cafe (£)
✉ 83, Victoria Street, Bunbury
☎ (08) 9791 4030

Taking in beautiful coastal scenery, this drive can just about be accomplished in a day – or you might want to stay overnight to fully appreciate the area.

Leave Perth via the Stirling Highway, then follow Cockburn Road and Patterson Road to Rockingham.

Make a brief stop at Rockingham, an attractive seaside resort offering excellent beaches and the chance to see fairy penguins at Penguin Island.

Continue south on the Mandurah Road.

Located on the coast at the mouth of idyllic Peel Inlet, Mandurah is the perfect spot for swimming, fishing and boating. There is a wildlife park, a miniature village, and swimming with dolphins in summer.

Continue south on the Old Coast Road.

Yalgorup National Park offers a peaceful environment of swamps, lakes, dunes and woodland. Birdwatchers should look out for some of the 100 or so species of waterbird that frequent the area.

Continue south.

The resort town of Bunbury offers sandy beaches, a harbour and the chance to meet some wild dolphins

The popular seaside resort of Bunbury has good beaches and a harbour, and you might well see dolphins at Koombana Beach, where the Dolphin Discovery Centre is located. You can drive further south to see the tall 400-year-old trees of the Tuart Forest National Park. If you wish to stay in the area overnight, continue to Busselton and Margaret River (➤ 88).

Head back towards Perth on the fast South Western Highway.

Returning to Perth, stop at the historic town of Armadale (History House Museum), 30km from the city, the Araluen Botanic Park at Roleystone, and Cohunu Koala Park at Gosnells.

Continue on to Perth.

Where To...

Eat and Drink	92–99
Stay	100–103
Shop	104–109
Take Children	110–11
Be Entertained	112–16

Above: *Sandstone gorge on the Murchison River in Kalbarri National Park, Western Australia*
Right: *look out for koalas!*

New South Wales & Australian Capital Territory

Prices
The recommended restaurants on these pages are classified into three price categories. Prices are for a three-course meal for one person, without drinks or service charge.

£ = under $A30
££ = $A31–49
£££ = over $A50

Eating out in Australia
Although Australia has its share of expensive restaurants, eating out is generally reasonably priced, and you can sample cuisines from all over the world. Restaurants fall into two major types: licensed to serve alcohol, or the popular BYO category – Bring Your Own wine, beer or other liquor. Booking is recommended for most restaurants, and most are non-smoking (except for outdoor areas). There is generally no service charge, although a GST (Goods and Services Tax) of 10 per cent is added to bills, and tipping is optional.

New South Wales

Sydney

Bayswater Brasserie (££)
This stylish brasserie offers Modern Australian food and also has the benefits of a bar and garden seating.
32 Bayswater Road, Kings Cross (02) 9357 2177 Lunch Fri, dinner Mon–Sat Kings Cross

Catalina (£££)
Right on the harbour, with a fabulous view, outdoor area and fine seafood.
1 Sunderland Avenue, Rose Bay (02) 9371 0555 Lunch daily, dinner Mon–Sat 324, 325

Chinta Ria Temple of Love (££)
Good-value Malaysian food in this lively Darling Harbour restaurant.
Roof Terrace, Cockle Bay Wharf, Darling Harbour (02) 9264 3211 Lunch and dinner daily Monorail: Darling Park

Doyle's on the Beach (££–£££)
Sydney's most famous seafood restaurant, with a wonderful harbour view.
11 Marine Parade, Watsons Bay (02) 9337 2007 Lunch & dinner daily 324, 325

MCA Café (££)
Located in the Museum of Contemporary Art, this all-day café offers good Modern Australian cuisine and a great view of the harbour and Opera House.
140 George Street, The Rocks (02) 9214 4253 Lunch and dinner daily Circular Quay

Tetsuya's (£££)
This high-class restaurant blends French, Japanese and Australian food in award-winning combinations.
529 Kent Street (02) 9267 2900 Dinner Tue–Sat Town Hall

Blue Mountains

Café Bon Ton (£–££)
This lively café serves everything from breakfasts to lunch to three-course dinners. There is a large outdoor area, and a log fire burns in winter.
192 The Mall, Leura (02) 4782 4377 All day Wed–Mon. No dinner Tue Leura

Darley's (£££)
Arguably the best restaurant in the Blue Mountains. Fine Modern Australian dining, in a historic building.
Lilianfels Blue Mountains, Lilianfels Avenue, Katoomba (02) 4780 1200 Dinner daily Katoomba

Byron Bay

Fins (£££)
This award-winning seafood restaurant represents Byron Bay's finest dining experience. There is also an excellent wine list.
Beach Hotel, corner of Jonson and Bay streets (02) 6685 5029 Dinner daily None

Coffs Harbour

Tide & Pilot (££)
A lively brasserie near the marina that specialises in seafood. There are great views of the water.
Marina Drive (02) 6651 6888 Lunch & dinner daily None

Hunter Valley

The Cellar Restaurant (££–£££)

Fine Modern Australian fare in a cosy setting – dine beside a log fire in winter.

Hunter Valley Gardens Village, Broke Road, Pokolbin (02) 4998 7584 Lunch daily, dinner Mon–Sat None

Robert's at Pepper Tree (£££)

Specialising in country-style food, this delightful establishment is surrounded by Hunter Valley vineyards.

Halls Road, Pokolbin (02) 4998 7330 Lunch & dinner daily None

Lord Howe Island

Arajilla (££)

One of the best on Lord Howe, this restaurant offers fine, innovative food.

Arajilla Retreat, Old Settlement Beach (02) 6563 2002 Dinner daily None

Southern Highlands

Heritage Restaurant (£££)

One of the area's best restaurants – specialising in Modern Australian dishes prepared from the best local produce.

Mercure Grand Hotel, 9 Kangaloon Road, Bowral (02) 4861 4833 Lunch Sat–Sun, dinner daily None

Janeks Café (£)

Small, lively café, offering good value, from breakfasts through lunch and afternoon tea.

Corbett Plaza, Wingecarribee Street, Bowral (02) 4861 4414 Lunch daily Bowral

Canberra & the Australian Capital Territory

Canberra City

Anise (££)

An acclaimed Modern Australian restaurant in central Canberra. Elegant decor and fine service complement the meat, fish and game dishes.

Melbourne Building, West Row, Canberra City (02) 6257 0700 Lunch Tue–Fri, dinner Tue–Sat Any City Centre bus

Gus' Cafe (£)

This tiny Canberra institution is a great, cheap place for excellent coffee, snacks, and main meals like pasta and seafood.

Shop 8, Garema Place, Bunda Street, Canberra City (02) 6248 8118 Daily 7:30AM–late Any City Centre bus

Ottoman Cuisine (££)

This highly acclaimed Turkish restaurant offers something different. Specialising in seafood, it is one of Canberra's hottest dining spots.

Corner Blackall and Broughton Streets, Barton (02) 6273 6111 Lunch Tue–Fri, dinner Tue–Sat 39

The Tryst (££)

In the popular Manuka dining precinct, this brasserie offers everything from Asian to Mediterranean dishes, as well as an excellent wine list.

Bougainville Street, Manuka (02) 6239 4422 Lunch and dinner daily 39

Modern Australian Cuisine

Acclaimed by 'foodies' the world over, Modern Australian cuisine has its roots in the nation's multiculturalism. By using the freshest produce and combining cuisines as varied as Thai and Mediterranean, Australian chefs are creating taste sensations in every major city. 'Bush tucker' – consisting of ingredients generally considered traditional Aboriginal fare – is also popular, and you can sample unusual delicacies like native berries, crocodile, kangaroo and emu.

Queensland

Australian Seafood
With an extraordinary range of produce from the sea, it is not surprising that Australia boasts so many excellent seafood restaurants. Every major city offers at least a couple of really good places that serve this cuisine, and many coastal towns have their own specialities. Tuna from South Australia, Tasmania's Atlantic salmon, Sydney rock oysters, Brisbane's Moreton Bay bugs, and the tropical fish, barramundi, are all highly recommended.

Brisbane

Baguette (££–£££)
An established and renowned restaurant with a menu that exhibits French, Australian and Asian influences.
150 Racecourse Road, Ascot
(07) 3268 6168
Lunch & dinner daily
300, 303

City Gardens Café (£–££)
Set in Brisbane's lush Botanic Gardens, this delightful café serves coffees and delicious meals and snacks.
City Botanic Gardens, Alice Street **(07) 3229 1554** **Breakfast, lunch & afternoon tea daily** **The Loop**

E'cco Bistro (£££)
One of Brisbane's hottest restaurants, E'cco serves acclaimed modern-style dishes in a small but lively setting.
100 Boundary Street
(07) 3831 8344 **Lunch Tue–Fri, dinner Tue–Sat**
The Loop

Fix Bar & Restaurant (£–££)
A city centre pub bistro with incredibly good value meals and snacks, as well as an excellent wine list.
The Port Office Hotel, Edward /Margaret streets
(07) 3210 6016
Lunch & dinner daily
The Loop

Gertie's Bar & Restaurant (££)
This popular eatery offers tapas and Modern Australian dishes – and it's also a great place for people watching!
699 Brunswick Street, New Farm **(07) 3358 5088**
Lunch & dinner daily
190, 194

Kookaburra River Queens (££)
Although perfectly acceptable, the food isn't the highlight. Here you can enjoy a cruise, complete with live entertainment, along the tranquil Brisbane River.
Departs from Eagle Street Pier, Eagle Street **(07) 3221 1300** **Lunch & dinner daily**
The Loop

Michael's Riverside (£££)
In a prime riverfront position with wonderful views, this popular restaurant offers Mediterranean and international cuisine.
Riverside Centre, 123 Eagle Street **(07) 3832 5522**
Lunch Mon–Fri, dinner daily
The Loop

Tropical North Queensland

Catalina Restaurant (£££)
With its Australian and Asian cuisine and delightful veranda seating, this Port Douglas eatery is a winner.
22 Wharf Street, Port Douglas **(07) 4099 5287**
Dinner Tue–Sun **None**

Fishlips Bar and Grill (££)
A wonderful seafood menu, including local barramundi. This is one of the best places to eat in Cairns.
228 Sheridan Street, Cairns
(07) 4041 1700 **Lunch Fri, dinner daily** **None**

Perrotta's at the Gallery (£)
This art gallery eatery has a varied and interesting menu, and, as a bonus, there are

great views of the ocean from its outside seating. The low prices too are an added attraction.

Regional Art Gallery, Corner Abbott and Shields Streets, Cairns (07) 4031 5899 Lunch & dinner daily None

Nautilus (£££)
Fine seafood is the speciality of this glamorous tropical restaurant, set in a rainforest environment.

17 Murphy Street, Port Douglas (07) 4099 5330 Dinner daily None

Red Ochre Grill (££)
You can sample a variety of unusual Aussie bush tucker here, from a menu that includes crocodile and almost 40 other native foodstuffs.

43 Shields Street, Cairns (07) 4051 0100 Lunch Mon–Sat, dinner daily None

Gold Coast

Ristorante Fellini (££)
A popular family-run Italian restaurant, featuring hand-made pasta, seafood and meat dishes and wonderful views.

Marina Mirage, Seaworld Drive, Main Beach (07) 5531 0300 Lunch and dinner daily 1, 1A

RPR's Restaurant (£££)
An elegant hotel dining room that is famous for its Modern Australian cuisine, including seafood and kangaroo dishes.

Royal Pines Resort, Ross Street, Ashmore (07) 5597 1111 or 1800 074 999 Dinner Tue–Sat 1, 1A, 18

Salty Plum (££)
A fine restaurant, offering an innovative Modern Australian menu in pleasant modern surroundings.

Oasis Shopping Centre, Beachside, Broadbeach (07) 5531 5699 Lunch & dinner daily 1, 1A

Sunshine Coast

Aromas (£–££)
An all-day bistro, serving everything from cakes and excellent coffee to Mediterranean-style lunches and dinners. A great spot for people watching!

32 Hastings Street, Noosa Heads (07) 5474 9788 Breakfast, lunch and dinner daily None

Lindoni's Ristorante (££)
With its fine traditional food and wines, this is the Sunshine Coast's best Italian restaurant.

Hastings Street, Noosa Heads (07) 5447 5111 Dinner daily None

Ricky Ricardos (££–£££)
One of Noosa's favourite eateries, this comfortable restaurant serves modern-style dishes in a delightful riverside setting.

Noosa Wharf, Quamby Place, Noosa Heads (07) 5447 2455 Lunch and dinner daily None

The Spirit House (££)
Although it's located inland from the coast, this superb Asian-style restaurant, in a unique rainforest setting, is well worth a visit.

4 Ninderry Road, Yandina (07) 5446 8994 Lunch daily, dinner Wed–Sat None

Asian Cuisines
Australia's proximity to Asia, and the fact that the country has a substantial Asian population, have led to oriental food becoming extremely popular. Generally, Indian restaurants are not as good as in many other parts of the world, but there are plenty of high-quality Thai, Indonesian, Malaysian, Korean, Japanese, Vietnamese, Chinese and other Asian eateries in which to enjoy these exotic cuisines.

Victoria & Tasmania

Melbourne's Restaurants
Although Sydney would dispute the claim, Melbourne likes to regard itself as Australia's culinary capital. There are some 4,000 restaurants, and dining out is a favourite Melbourne pastime. With 170 or so ethnic groups among the city's population, the variety of cuisines is extraordinary – everything from Spanish to Korean is represented – and there are prices to suit every budget.

Victoria

Melbourne

Blue Train Café (£–££)
A reasonably priced café in the riverside Southgate shopping and dining complex. The wood-fired pizzas are worth trying.
Mid West Level, Southgate, Southbank (03) 969 0011 Lunch & dinner daily City Circle tram

Café Di Stasio (££–£££)
Popular Italian restaurant serving hand-made pasta and fine meat and seafood dishes.
31 Fitzroy Street, St Kilda (03) 9525 3999 Lunch & dinner daily Any St Kilda tram

Donovans (££–£££)
In a wonderful position on St Kilda's seafront, Donovans serves superb Italian fare in elegant surroundings.
40 Jacka Boulevard, St Kilda (03) 9534 8221 Lunch & dinner daily Any St Kilda tram

Flower Drum (£££)
This high-quality Chinese restaurant offers an unusual menu that has received many accolades.
17 Market Lane (03) 9662 3655 Lunch Mon–Sat, dinner daily City Circle tram

Hairy Canary (££)
This trendy city-centre café is a good spot for breakfast, coffee, lunch or dinner. Main meals include tapas, pasta and some great risotto dishes.
212 Little Collins Street (03) 9654 2471 Breakfast, lunch & dinner daily Any Swanston Street tram

Nudel Bar (£)
A good-value café serving noodles of all varieties, from Asian to Italian, with a range of sauces.
76 Bourke Street (03) 9662 9100 Lunch & dinner daily City Circle tram

Il Solito Posto (£–££)
Excellent Italian fare on two levels – a downstairs dining room, and a cheaper bistro.
Shop 4, 113 Collins Street (03) 9654 4466 Lunch & dinner Mon–Sat City Circle tram

Ballarat

The Ansonia (££)
Excellent modern Australian fare in a smart boutique hotel.
32 Lydiard Street South (03) 5332 4678 Breakfast, lunch & dinner daily Ballarat

Great Ocean Road

Chris's Beacon Point Restaurant (££–£££)
This restaurant serves innovative seafood and Greek-influenced meals, and has a superb ocean view.
280 Skenes Creek Road, Skenes Creek, near Apollo Bay (03) 5237 6411 Lunch & dinner daily None

The Victoria Hotel (££)
This beautifully renovated pub offers both a casual café and more formal dining room, both serving good Modern Australian cuisine.
42 Bank Street, Port Fairy (03) 5568 2891 Lunch & dinner daily None

Phillip Island

The Jetty (££)
Phillip Island's premier restaurant offers fine local lobster and other seafood.

The Esplanade, Cowes (03) 5952 2060 Lunch Sat–Sun, dinner daily None

Tasmania

Hobart

Annapurna (£–££)
Excellent Indian meals, including good vegetarian food, at very reasonable prices. Very popular, so booking is advisable.
305 Elizabeth Street, North Hobart (03) 6236 9500 Lunch Mon–Fri, dinner daily None

Lebrina (££–£££)
Just north of the city centre and offering some of Hobart's best European cuisine.
155 New Town Road, New Town (03) 6228 7775 Dinner Tue–Sat None

Maldini (££)
In the heart of bustling Salamanca Place, this popular café offers great coffee and a range of good Italian meals.
47 Salamanca Place (03) 6223 4460 Breakfast, lunch & dinner daily None

Mures Upper Deck (££–£££)
Hobart's best known restaurant offers a wonderful range of seafood, a lively atmosphere, and good waterfront views.
Mures Fish Centre, Victoria Dock (03) 6231 1999 Lunch & dinner daily None

Panache (£–££)
Another excellent Salamanca café, serving well-priced Modern Australian dishes – from soup and salads to gourmet sandwiches, featuring home-made bread.
89 Salamanca Place (03) 6224 2929 Lunch & dinner Mon–Sat None

Devonport

The Gingerbread House (££)
Devonport's classiest restaurant offers a fine seasonal à la carte menu.
71 Wright Street (03) 6427 0466 Lunch & dinner daily None

Launceston

Fee and Me (££–£££)
One of Tasmania's best Modern Australian restaurants.
190 Charles Street (03) 6331 3195 Dinner Mon–Sat None

Star Bar Café (£–££)
An ideal place for a snack, coffee and cake, or a good-value main meal. There is also a bar.
113 Charles Street (03) 6331 6111 Lunch & dinner daily None

Port Arthur

Felons Restaurant (££)
This à la carte restaurant in the Visitor Centre creates innovative dishes made from the best local produce.
Port Arthur Historic Site, Port Arthur 1800 659 101 or (03) 6251 2310 Dinner daily None

Strahan

Franklin Manor (££–£££)
A surprisingly upmarket restaurant for this small west-coast town.
The Esplanade (03) 6471 7311 Dinner daily None

Tasmanian Produce
Among Australia's array of fresh, flavoursome produce that has had such a strong influence on the acclaimed Modern Australian cuisine, Tasmania's home-grown products stand out. There is wonderful seafood such as Atlantic salmon, ocean trout and crayfish; superb Bries, Camemberts and other gourmet cheeses; fine meats; and fruit and vegetables with real taste. To wash it all down, Tasmania's excellent wines are some of Australia's finest.

South Australia & Northern Territory

'Tourist Restaurants'
Australia's major cities all have an array of dining options particularly designed for tourists. Many such restaurants are in scenic locations, and though the standard of cuisine is not always out of the ordinary, it's worth sampling a few. You can dine while cruising Sydney Harbour or the Brisbane River, or at the top of tall buildings with spectacular views; and you can sample Aussie 'bush tucker' in most capital cities.

South Australia

Adelaide

Blake's (£££)
An elegant, central hotel restaurant with an innovative Modern Australian menu. Good service.
Hyatt Regency Adelaide, North Terrace (08) 8238 2381 Lunch Fri, dinner Mon & Wed–Sat City Loop

Botanic Cafe (££)
An unusual Modern Italian menu, a good wine list and views over the parklands.
4 East Terrace (08) 8232 0626 Lunch Tue–Fri & Sun, dinner Tue–Sat City Loop

The Oxford (££)
A long-running pub restaurant, serving Modern Australian dishes that are deservedly popular with Adelaide locals.
101 O'Connell Street, North Adelaide (08) 8267 2652 Lunch Mon–Fri, dinner Mon–Sat 182, 222

Adelaide Hills

Bridgewater Mill (£££)
One of Australia's best. Modern Australian cuisine in a historic gold flour mill.
Mount Barker Road, Bridgewater (08) 8339 3422 Lunch Thur–Mon None

Barossa Valley

1918 Bistro and Grill (££)
Delicious country-style food is the speciality of this rustic restaurant in the heart of the Barossa Valley.
94 Murray Street, Tanunda (08) 8563 0405 Lunch & dinner daily None

Kangaroo Island

Ozone Seafront Hotel (££)
A family bistro with a wide variety of food served from breakfast to dinner.
The Foreshore, Kingscote (08) 8553 2011 Breakfast, lunch & dinner daily None

Northern Territory

Darwin

Cornucopia Museum Café (££)
Located in Darwin's premier museum, right on the waterfront, this excellent daytime café offers good-value meals.
Conacher Street, Bullocky Point (08) 8981 1002 Brunch & lunch daily None

The Hanuman (££–£££)
Acclaimed Thai and Nonya (Malaysian) cuisine in an elegant setting.
28 Mitchell Street (08) 8941 3500 Lunch Mon–Fri, dinner daily None

Alice Springs

Bluegrass Restaurant (££)
One of Alice's best restaurants, offering a wide variety of dishes – everything from kangaroo to vegetarian meals, seafood and pastas.
Corner of Todd Street & Stott Terrace (08) 8955 5188 Lunch & dinner Wed–Mon None

Uluru

Most of the Ayers Rock Resort restaurants, bars and cafés are within the main hotels – such as the very good Sails in the Desert (➤ 103).

Western Australia

Western Australia

Perth

Dusit Thai (££)

Perth's Northbridge dining area is full of good restaurants – including this established Thai eatery.

249 James Street, Northbridge (08) 9328 7647 Lunch Tue–Fri, dinner Tue–Sun Central Area Transit bus

44 King Street (££)

Right in the city centre, this brasserie serves a wide range of snacks and main meals, most of which are Mediterranean inspired.

44 King Street (08) 9321 4476 Breakfast, lunch & dinner daily Central Area Transit bus

Fraser's (££–£££)

Top city and river views, good service and an imaginative Modern Australian menu are on offer here.

Fraser Avenue, Kings Park, West Perth (08) 9481 7100 Breakfast, lunch & dinner daily 33

The Loose Box (£££)

A half-hour drive from the city, this is arguably Western Australia's best restaurant with classic French cuisine. Award-winning venue with overnight accommodation in luxury cottages.

6825 Great Eastern Highway, Mundaring (08) 9295 1787 Lunch Sun, dinner Wed–Sat None

Albany

Ristorante Leonardo's (££)

Serving pastas and Italian steak, vegetarian and seafood dishes, this is one of Albany's most popular restaurants.

164 Stirling Terrace (08) 9841 1732 Dinner Mon–Sat None

Bunbury

Louisa's (££)

This delightful restaurant in a heritage building offers a Modern Australian menu.

15 Clifton Street (08) 9721 9959 Dinner Mon–Sat None

Fremantle

Essex Restaurant (££)

Specialising in steaks and seafood, in a delightful 100-year-old cottage.

20 Essex Streeet (08) 9335 5725 Lunch Wed–Fri, Sun; dinner daily Fremantle

The Red Herring (££)

In a riverside setting, this classy Modern Australian restaurant offers excellent seafood.

26 Riverside Road, East Fremantle (08) 9339 1611 Lunch & dinner daily Fremantle

Kalgoorlie-Boulder

Judds Restaurant (££)

Pub restaurant overlooking Kalgoorlie's main street offers good-value meals. The specialty is woodfired pizza.

The Kalgoorlie Hotel, 319 Hannan Street (08) 9021 3046 Lunch & dinner daily None

Margaret River

Leeuwin Estate Winery Restaurant (££)

With an emphasis on fresh local produce, this elegant but casual restaurant offers Modern Australian dishes.

Stevens Road (08) 9759 0000 Lunch daily, dinner Sat None

The Café Scene

Australia's thriving café scene provides plenty of options for inexpensive dining. Every capital city, and many of the larger towns, have lively cafés that serve snacks and light meals for $10 or less. Many of these eateries have outdoor dining areas – often as simple as a few pavement tables – which are wonderful for the warmer months, and you will generally find excellent coffee to accompany your meal.

New South Wales & Canberra

Prices
The recommended hotels on these pages are classified into three price categories. Prices are per room per night, regardless of single or double occupancy.

£	**= under $A120**
££	**= $A120 – 240**
£££	**= over $A250**

Accommodation in Australia
Australia offers a wide variety of accommodation. There are world-class city hotels like Sydney's Park Hyatt, and luxurious island resorts such as Queensland's Hayman Island. You can stay on working farms to experience country and Outback life, or book into a historic Tasmanian cottage for bed and breakfast. Cheaper options are motels and Aussie hotels – functional yet often atmospheric pubs.

New South Wales

Sydney

Hotel Ibis Darling Harbour (££)
This hotel has great views, a popular restaurant and a waterfront location.
www.accorhotels.com 70 Murray Street, Darling Harbour (02) 9563 0888 Convention

Park Hyatt Sydney (£££)
One of Sydney's very best hotels, located opposite the Opera House.
www.sydney.park.hyatt.com 7 Hickson Road, The Rocks (02) 9241 1234 431–434

The Russell (££)
This small Victorian hotel has individual rooms, a roof garden and is close to the Rocks and city centre.
www.therussell.com.au 143a George Street, The Rocks (02) 9241 3543 Circular Quay

Blue Mountains

The Mountain Heritage (££–£££)
This historic hotel offers an ideal location, superb views and a range of good-value accommodation.
www.mountainheritage.com.au Apex/Lovel streets, Katoomba (02) 4782 2155, Katoomba

Coffs Harbour

Break Free Aanuka Beach Resort (£££)
Set on a sandy beach, this attractive hotel offers suites furnished with antiques, and delightful gardens
www.breakfree.com.au Firman Drive, Diggers Beach (02) 6652 7555, Coffs Harbour

Hunter Valley

Peppers Convent (£££)
One of the Hunter Valley's best hotels, the historic Convent provides spacious rooms that open onto a veranda. There is an outdoor pool and tennis courts.
www.peppers.com.au Halls Road, Pokolbin (02) 4998 7764 Pokolbin

Lord Howe Island

Somerset Apartments (££)
This large self-catering lodge set among tropical gardens has pleasant, well-equipped units, each with a private veranda, which all makes for a relaxing stay.
www.lordhoweisle.com.au Neds Beach Road (02) 6563 2061 None

Canberra

Forrest Inn and Apartments (£–££)
Located close to Parliament House and the lively Manuka restaurant precinct, these comfortable motel rooms and serviced apartments represent very good value.
www.forrestinn.com.au 30 National Circuit, Forrest (02) 6295 3433 39

Hyatt Hotel Canberra (£££)
This is indisputably the national capital's finest (also most expensive) hotel, in a great location close to most of the city's main attractions. The renovated 1920s building is charming, the rooms are spacious, and there are extensive, well-maintained gardens in which to relax.
www.canberra.park.hyatt.com Commonwealth Avenue, Yarralumla (02) 6270 1234, 31, 39

Queensland & Victoria

Queensland

Brisbane

Holidy Inn Brisbane (££)
Good value in a convenient city-centre location – large rooms, two restaurants, bars, a sauna and a gym.
www.brisbane.holiday-inn.com
✉ Roma Street ☎ (07) 3238 2222 🚉 Roma Street Station

Stamford Plaza Brisbane (£££)
A luxurious hotel on the waterfront and close to the Botanic Gardens.
www.stamford.com.au
✉ Corner Edward and Margaret Streets ☎ (07) 3221 1999 🚌 The Loop

Cairns

Hotel Sofitel Reef Casino Cairns (£££)
Part of the Cairns casino complex, this hotel provides all the expected luxuries and a few more besides.
www.reefcasino.com.au
✉ 35–41 Wharf Street
☎ (07) 4030 8801
🚌 None

Gold Coast

Paros on the Beach (££)
Right on the beach, Paros has 35 Mediterranean-style apartments.
www.parosonthebeach.com
✉ 26 Old Burleigh Road, Surfers Paradise ☎ (07) 5592 0780 🚌 1, 1A

Sunshine Coast

Netanya Noosa (££)
This delightful low-rise resort, on the beachfront, offers luxury and relaxation at an affordable price.
www.netanyanoosa.com.au
✉ 75 Hastings Street, Noosa Heads ☎ (07) 5447 4722, 🚌 None

Victoria

Melbourne

Novotel St Kilda (££)
This large, hotel on Port Phillip Bay includes a spa, gymnasium and heated pool.
www.novotelstkilda.com.au
✉ 16 The Esplanade, St Kilda ☎ (03) 9525 5522 🚌 Any St Kilda tram

Sheraton Towers Southgate (£££)
One of Melbourne's best hotels, this modern establishment rises above the Southgate dining and entertainment precinct.
www.sheraton-towers.com.au
✉ 1 Southgate Avenue, Southbank ☎ (03) 8696 8888 🚌 City Circle tram

The Victoria Hotel (£–££)
In a convenient location behind the Town Hall, the historic Victoria offers extremely good value.
www.victoriahotel.com.au
✉ 215 Little Collins Street ☎ (03) 9653 0441 🚌 Any Swanston Walk tram

Great Ocean Road

Cumberland Lorne Resort (£££)
An apartment-style resort, ideal for exploring the Great Ocean Road.
www.cumberland.com.au
✉ 150 Mountjoy Parade, Lorne ☎ (03) 5289 2400 🚌 None

Phillip Island

Kaloha Holiday Resort (££)
Located in the main town of Cowes, the resort offers self-contained units.
www.kaloha.com.au
✉ Corner of Steele & Chapel Streets, Cowes ☎ (03) 5952 2179

Queensland's Island Resorts
In addition to the Queensland accommodation detailed here, there are many island resorts close to, or even on, the Great Barrier Reef. From the sophisticated luxury of Lizard Island to the family-oriented resorts on islands like South Molle in the Whitsunday region, there is something for every taste and budget. You can also stay right on the reef – Heron and Lady Elliot islands are the best bets.

Tasmania & South Australia

Serviced Apartments
Serviced apartments are a very popular accommodation option. These self-catering units offer from one to three bedrooms, and generally have a separate lounge/kitchen area. Such apartments are usually much cheaper than hotels of a comparable standard, and are ideal for families, small groups or those who just want the freedom to cook 'at home'.

Tasmania

Hobart

Corus Hotel Hobart (££)
Good value in a central Hobart location. The hotel has pleasant rooms, plus a bar and restaurant.
www.corushotels.com.au
156 Bathurst Street (03) 6232 6255 None

Somerset on the Pier (£££)
A luxurious hotel with loft-style bedrooms. The waterfront setting, on a 1930s pier, is superb.
www.the-ascott.com
Elizabeth Street Pier
(03) 6220 6600 None

Freycinet Peninsula

Freycinet Lodge (££–£££)
Set in Freycinet National Park, this timber lodge offers total tranquillity. Guests stay in comfortably furnished cabins that feature a private balcony. The lodge also has a tennis court and restaurant.
Freycinet National Park, Coles Bay (03) 6257 0101, www.freycinetlodge.com.au
None

Launceston

The Old Bakery Inn (££)
A beautifully restored inn. Accommodation includes converted stables, a cottage or the old bakery itself.
270 York Street (03) 6331 7900, www.bestwestern.com.au None

Strahan

Franklin Manor (£££)
This small, welcoming hotel is the pick of the West Coast accommodation.
The Esplanade
(03) 6471 7311, www.franklinmanor.com.au
None

South Australia

Adelaide

Hyatt Regency Adelaide (£££)
Adelaide's best hotel, right in the heart of the city.
www.adelaide.hyatt.com.au
North Terrace (08) 8231 1234 City Loop or 99B

Quest Mansions (££)
The Quest Mansions offers spacious self-contained apartments in a centrally located historic building.
www.questapartments.com.au
21 Pulteney Street
(08) 8232 0033 City Loop

Barossa Valley

Novotel Barossa Valley Resort (££–£££)
This large resort provides superb facilities, including tennis courts and a nearby 18-hole golf course.
www.novotelbarossa.com
Golf Links Road, Rowland Flat (08) 8524 0000
Bluebird Barossa Train to Tanunda

Flinders Ranges

Wilpena Pound Resort (£–££)
In the heart of the Ranges, this resort provides motel-style rooms, caravans and powered campsites.
www.wilpenapound.com.au
Wilpena Pound (08) 8648 0004 None

Kangaroo Island

Ozone Seafront Hotel (££)
Set on the seafront, the Ozone is one of the island's best hotels.
www.ozonehotel.com
The Foreshore, Kingscote
(08) 8553 2011
None

Northern Territory & Western Australia

Northern Territory

Darwin

City Gardens Apartments (££)
Reasonably priced apartments and family units, close to the centre of Darwin. The hotel has a pool.
www.citygardensapts.com.au
93 Woods Street (08) 8941 2888 None

Holiday Inn Esplanade Darwin (£££)
One of Darwin's best hotels, including a restaurant, gymnasium and pool.
www.ichotelsgroup.com
122 The Esplanade
(08) 8980 0800
None

Alice Springs

Alice Springs Resort (££–£££)
This pleasant resort hotel offers a variety of accommodation, from family rooms to a more luxurious standard.
www.voyages.com.au
34 Stott Terrace (02) 9339 1030 None

Katherine

Mercure Inn Katherine (££)
Frontier offers comfortable motel-style rooms and budget caravans.
www.accorhotels.com
Stuart Highway (08) 8972 1744 None

Uluru

Sails in the Desert (£££)
With its distinctive architecture and excellent facilities, this is the best place to stay in the Uluru area.
www.voyages.com.au
Yulara Drive, Ayers Rock Resort (02) 9339 1030
None

Western Australia

Perth

Hyatt Regency Perth (£££)
Located beside the Swan River, this luxurious hotel is among the best in Perth.
www.hyatt.com
99 Adelaide Terrace
(08) 9225 1234 Central Area Transit bus

Riverview on Mount Street (££)
Situated close to the city centre and Kings Park, this hotel consists of self-contained studio apartments.
www.riverview.com.au
42 Mount Street (08) 9321 8963, Central Area Transit bus

Kalgoorlie-Boulder

Mercure Hotel Plaza Kalgoorlie (££)
Kalgoorlie's best hotel offers modern comfort and good facilities.
www.accorhotels.com.au
45 Egan Street (08) 9021 4544, None

The Kimberley

El Questro Wilderness Park (£–£££)
This vast cattle station provides everything from campsites and bungalows to luxurious rooms.
www.elquestro.com.au
Gibb River Road, via Kununurra (08) 9169 1777
El Questro Wilderness Park

Margaret River

Cape Lodge (£££)
An award-winning lodge with colonial furniture, airy rooms and a rural atmosphere.
www.capelodge.com.au
Caves Road, Yallingup
(08) 9755 6311
None

Wilderness Accommodation
Many of the continent's most scenic regions – national parks like Kakadu and the Flinders Ranges, the World Heritage sites of the Tasmanian wilderness and some of the Great Barrier Reef islands – have little in the way of hotel accommodation. You can, however, camp for a small fee in many of these parks and reserves, while others provide basic but cosy cabins and huts.

Australiana & Aboriginal Crafts

Opening Hours
Australian shops offer an excellent range of goods and relatively competitive prices – Sydney and Melbourne in particular have a wide variety of retail outlets, selling everything from designer clothing to high-quality souvenirs. Shopping hours are generally 9–5:30 on weekdays and 9–5 on Saturdays. Most large stores and suburban shopping centres are also open on Sundays, and each capital city offers late shopping on one night.

Australiana

New South Wales

Done Art & Design
Ken Done's incredibly popular and colourful designs are found on beachwear, T-shirts, accessories and homewares.
123 George Street, The Rocks, Sydney (02) 9251 6099 Circular Quay

RM Williams
This is the original 'Bushman's Outfitters', where you can buy Akubra hats, Drizabone oilskin coats and country-style clothing.
389 George Street, Sydney (02) 9262 2228 Town Hall

SOH Store
Located in the Lower Concourse of the Opera House and stocking a wide range of Sydney Opera House related and themed gifts and souvenirs.
Sydney Opera House, Bennelong Point, Sydney (02) 9251 7772 Circular Quay

Australian Capital Territory

Australian Choice
This shop sells only good Australian-made products, and is great for gifts and souvenirs.
Canberra Centre, Bunda Street, Canberra City (02) 6257 5315 Any city-centre bus

Queensland

Australian Woolshed
This major attraction (➤ 110) includes an excellent store, which offers high-quality Australian gifts and souvenirs.
148 Samford Road, Ferny Hills, Brisbane (07) 3872 1100 Ferny Grove

Victoria

Body Map Australia
This excellent outlet sells a wide range of Australiana and Australian-made products – from T-shirts to souvenirs of all types.
Shop 107, Melbourne Central, 211 La Trobe Street, Melbourne (03) 9662 2900 City Circle tram

Chapel Street
Australian designer fashions are well represented on this lively street that stretches through a couple of inner-city suburbs.
South Yarra and Prahran, Melbourne Trams 6, 8, 72

Tasmania

Naturally Tasmanian
One of Hobart's best souvenir shops, selling Aussie clothing, sheepskin products, homewares, local foodstuffs and much more.
59 Salamanca Place, Hobart (03) 6223 4248 None

South Australia

South Australian Museum
This museum shop is a good place to find some unusual Australian gifts and souvenirs.
North Terrace, Adelaide (08) 8207 7500 City Loop

Western Australia

London Court
This Tudor-style arcade – a tourist attraction in itself – offers a wide range of souvenir, gift and Australiana-style shops.
Between Hay Street Mall and St George's Terrace, Perth (08) 9261 6666 Central Area Transit bus

Aboriginal Crafts

New South Wales

Aboriginal & Tribal Art Centre
Offers a splendid array of high-quality Aboriginal paintings, carvings, gifts, jewellery and collectables.
✉ 117 George Street, The Rocks, Sydney ☎ (02) 9247 9625 Circular Quay

Gavala Aboriginal Cultural Centre
This c entral Sydney outlet specialises in authentic Aboriginal art, clothing, indigenous music and a good range of other unusual souvenirs.
✉ Shop 321, Harbourside, Darling Harbour, Sydney ☎ (02) 9212 7232 Harbourside monorail

Queensland

Queensland Aboriginal Creations
Stocks Aboriginal items of all kinds – from didgeridoos to woodcarvings.
✉ 199 Elizabeth Street, Brisbane ☎ (07) 3224 5730 The Loop

Victoria

Aboriginal Art Galleries of Australia
A fine gallery selling a wide variety of Aboriginal artworks, particularly from the Central Desert region.
✉ 35 Spring Street, Melbourne ☎ (03) 9654 2516 City Circle tram

Tasmania

Tiagarra Aboriginal Cultural Centre & Museum
An excellent Aboriginal centre and museum, which also sells good quality arts and crafts.
✉ Mersey Bluff, Bluff Road, Devonport ☎ (03) 6424 8250 None

South Australia

Gallerie Australis
This highly recommended outlet in Adelaide's top hotel sells quality Aboriginal arts, crafts and artefacts.
✉ Lower Forecourt Plaza, Hyatt Regency Adelaide, North Terrace, Adelaide ☎ (08) 8231 4111 City Loop

Tandanya Aboriginal Cultural Institute
This centre's gift shop is stocked with well-made Aboriginal artworks and artefacts.
✉ 253 Grenfell Street, Adelaide ☎ (08) 8224 3200 City Loop

Northern Territory

Framed
Featuring Aboriginal art, crafts, sculptures and gifts, this Darwin gallery is certainly worth visiting.
✉ 55 Stuart Highway, Stuart Park, Darwin ☎ (08) 8981 2994 None

The Original Dreamtime Art Gallery
At this large gallery you can buy Aboriginal themed clothing and jewellery, as well as carvings, pottery and other artefacts.
✉ 63 Todd Mall, Alice Springs ☎ (08) 8952 8861 None

Western Australia

Creative Native
One of Perth's best Aboriginal art centres, with everything from paintings to silk scarves and jewellery.
✉ 32 King Street, Perth ☎ (08) 9322 3398 Central Area Transit bus

Australian Made!
International products and labels are well represented, but there are some uniquely Australian purchases that are particularly appealing. Beachwear and designer T-shirts, such as those created by Ken Done and Mambo, are colourful and innovative, while Aussie 'bush clothing' is also popular. Other Australiana includes unusual Aboriginal-designed clothing and crafts, and home-grown products such as sheepskin items, designer knitwear, opals and South Sea pearls.

Jewellery, Stores & Shopping Centres

Opals, diamonds and pearls
Australia produces most of the world's opals, and Australian stones are considered to be of a particularly fine quality. You can buy either 'white', or the more expensive 'black' opals, unset or made up into beautiful jewellery. Other exclusive (and expensive) precious stone purchases – both from the north of Western Australia – are Argyle diamonds, available in white, champagne and pink varieties, and exquisite South Sea pearls.

Opals, Gems & Jewellery

New South Wales

Flame Opals
One of Sydney's best opal stockists offers a good range of stones, both unset and made up into fine jewellery.
119 George Street, The Rocks, Sydney (02) 9247 3446 Circular Quay

Hardy Brothers
This gem specialist sells fine opals, South Sea pearls and Argyle diamonds from Western Australia, as well as other precious items.
Skygarden, 77 Castlereagh Street, Sydney (02) 9232 2422 St James

Percy Marks Fine Gems
One of Sydney's oldest gem specialists, this store offers opals, Argyle diamonds and South Sea Pearls – all set in Australian hand-crafted jewellery.
60 Elizabeth Street, Sydney (02) 9233 1355 Martin Place

Queensland

Quilpie Opals
This leading opal specialist sells beautiful stones direct from its Queensland mines.
Lennons Plaza, 68 Queen Street, Brisbane (07) 3221 5789 The Loop

Victoria

Ashley Opals
This is one of the best places in Melbourne to buy opals, South Sea pearls and Argyle diamonds.
85 Collins Street, Melbourne (03) 9654 4866 City Circle tram

Johnston Opals
Opals and opal-set jewellery are a specialty of this long-established company.
124 Exhibition Street, Melbourne (03) 9650 7434 City Circle tram

Makers Mark Gallery
An upmarket outlet for beautifully crafted jewellery that incorporates exquisite Argyle diamonds and gems.
101 Collins Street, Melbourne (03) 9654 8488 City Circle Tram

Tasmania

Handmark Gallery
Find innovative hand-made jewellery at this classy Hobart gallery.
77 Salamanca Place, Hobart (03) 6223 7895 None

South Australia

The Opal Mine
South Australia produces 60 per cent of the world's opals, and this Adelaide outlet offers good-quality stones.
30 Gawler Place, Adelaide (08) 8223 4023 City Loop

Northern Territory

Paspaley Pearls
Northern Australian pearls – regarded as the world's finest – and other exquisite jewellery are sold here.
Corner Bennett Street and The Mall, Darwin (08) 8982 5555 None

Western Australia

Perth Mint
This museum of gold and minting has a shop that sells exclusive jewellery and gifts.
Corner Hay and Hill streets, East Perth (08) 9421 7223 Central Area Transit bus

Department Stores & Shopping Centres

New South Wales

David Jones

One of Australia's very best stores, glamorous 'DJs' operates from two enormous city-centre buildings.

Elizabeth Street and Market Street, Sydney 13 3357 or 9266 5544 St James

Queen Victoria Building

This vast 1890s building, with its stained glass and tiled floors, is a delightful place in which to shop. There are over 200 boutiques here.

Corner George, York and Market Streets, Sydney (02) 9264 9209 Town Hall

Australian Capital Territory

Canberra Centre

This three-level shopping centre is Canberra's biggest – it contains a branch of David Jones and other large stores.

Bunda Street, Canberra City (02) 6247 5611 Any city-centre bus

Queensland

Marina Mirage

A waterfront Gold Coast shopping centre that offers 80 speciality shops, boutiques and art galleries.

Seaworld Drive, Broadwater Spit, Main Beach, Gold Coast (07) 5577 0088 1, 1A

Victoria

The Block Arcade

Opened in 1892, this arcade contains 30 shops and has a European atmosphere.

Between 282 Collins Street and 100 Elizabeth Street, Melbourne (03) 9654 5244 City Circle tram

Melbourne Central

This vast complex includes the Myer Department Store and over 150 other speciality shops.

211 La Trobe Street, Melbourne (03) 9922 1100 City Circle tram

Tasmania

Salamanca Place

This street's old sandstone warehouses have been converted into a delightful shopping complex offering arts, crafts, woollen goods and souvenirs.

Salamanca Place, Hobart None

South Australia

Rundle Mall

Adelaide's mall is home to many shops and the city's major department stores.

Rundle Mall, Adelaide City Loop

Northern Territory

Smith Street Mall

Darwin's main shopping area offers everything from clothing shops to Aboriginal art galleries.

Smith Street Mall, Darwin None

Western Australia

Forrest Chase Shopping Plaza

This large, modern shopping centre is one of the best places to shop in Perth. Convenient for the station.

Murray Street, between Forrest Place and Barrack Street, Perth (08) 9322 9111 Central Area Transit bus

Duty- and Tax-free

Australia's duty- and tax-free prices are very competitive and compare favourably with those of Asian ports. Overseas visitors receive a discount of around 30 per cent on perfumes, cigarettes and alcohol, electrical and electronic equipment, jewellery, watches and other items. There are many duty-free shops in city centres and at the airports, and Australia even offers a facility for visitors to purchase duty-free goods on arrival at international airport terminals.

Visitors can also obtain a refund for the GST (Goods and Services Tax) paid on goods costing $300 or more. Details are available from the Australian Customs Service ((02) 6275 6666 or 1300 363263, www.customs.gov.au).

Markets

Out of Town
Although the best shopping is generally found in the centre of capital cities, many suburbs, and even regional towns, offer some fine shops. City suburbs that are particularly good for shopping include Sydney's Paddington (offbeat fashions) and Double Bay (expensive designer clothing), and Melbourne's South Yarra and Toorak. Country town shopping – particularly for antiques and crafts – is excellent in NSW's Blue Mountains and Southern Highlands.

New South Wales

Paddington Markets

This Saturday market is the best in Sydney. There are over 250 stalls selling clothes and arts and crafts, as well as good food and free entertainment.

Corner Oxford and Newcombe Streets, Paddington, Sydney (02) 9331 2923 380, L82

The Rocks Market

A lively Saturday and Sunday event in the heart of Sydney's tourist mecca.

Upper George Street, The Rocks, Sydney (02) 9240 8717 Circular Quay

Australian Capital Territory

Old Bus Depot Markets

On Sundays, this old Canberra bus depot is transformed into an undercover market. Hand-made goods and collectables are the main items.

49 Wentworth Avenue, Kingston, Canberra (02) 6292 8391 Sun 10–4 39

Queensland

Eagle Street Pier Craft Market

A Sunday city-centre market offering quality handcrafted goods such as clothes, arts and crafts and some great gifts.

Riverside Centre and Eagle Street Pier, Eagle Street, Brisbane (07) 3846 4500 The Loop

Victoria

Queen Victoria Market

This Melbourne institution is a large indoor market selling everything from foodstuffs to fashion clothing.

Corner Elizabeth and Victoria Streets, Melbourne (03) 9320 5822 Daily except Mon Tram 19, 57, 59

St Kilda Esplanade Art & Craft Market

This popular Sunday market offers over 200 stalls that sell only hand-crafted items.

The Esplanade, St Kilda, Melbourne (03) 9209 6777 Any St Kilda tram

Tasmania

Salamanca Market

This is the place to be in Hobart on Saturdays – an excellent market set against the historic backdrop of Salamanca Place.

Salamanca Place, Hobart (03) 6238 2843 None

South Australia

Central Market

Dating from 1870, this is mainly a produce market – but a fascinating place to wander around nonetheless.

Grote and Gouger Streets, Adelaide (08) 8203 7494 Tue, Thu–Sat. Closed public holidays City Loop

Northern Territory

Mindil Beach Sunset Markets

This evening market features arts and crafts, many tempting food stalls and free entertainment.

Mindil Beach, Darwin Apr–Oct, Thu & Sun None

Western Australia

Fremantle Markets

A National Trust classified indoor market that sells fresh produce, clothing and crafts.

84 South Terrace, Fremantle (08) 9335 2515 Fri–Sun Fremantle

Crafts & Antiques

New South Wales

Object

Specialising in unique Australian crafts and design work, this excellent store is conveniently located in the heart of The Rocks.

88 George Street, The Rocks, Sydney (02) 9247 7984 Circular Quay

Peppergreen Trading Co

The Southern Highlands region is packed with antiques shops, but this large establishment offers an outstanding range of goods.

Market Place, Berrima
(02) 4877 1488
None

Sydney Antique Centre

This large centre contains some 60 shops on two floors. The antiques range from jewellery to clocks, figurines, books and dolls.

531 South Dowling Street, Surry Hills, Sydney
(02) 9361 3244
378, 380

Australian Capital Territory

Cuppacumbalong Craft Centre

Located in a charming old homestead, this centre is the outlet for painters, potters, weavers and other craftspeople.

Naas Road, Tharwa
(02) 6237 5116 None

Queensland

Paddington Antique Centre

A good range of antiques is available, just 3km west of Brisbane's city centre.

167 Latrobe Terrace, Paddington, Brisbane
(07) 3369 8088
374, 375

Victoria

Convent Gallery

This magnificantly restored former nunnery is now home to fine art, sculpture, jewellery, food and wine.

Cnr Hill and Daly Streets, Daylesford (03) 5348 3211
None

Potoroo

Award-winning Melbourne outlet sells fine art and craftworks, including unusual ceramics and glassware.

Southgate, Southbank, Melbourne (03) 9690 9859
City Circle tram

Tasmania

Saddlers Court Gallery

The historic village of Richmond, just a 30-minute drive from Hobart, is full of crafts and antiques outlets, including this interesting collection of shops.

48–50 Bridge Street, Richmond (03) 6260 2132
Tasmanian Redline from Hobart

South Australia

JamFactory Contemporary Craft and Design Centre

This old Adelaide food factory is an excellent place to find South Australian designed jewellery, and crafts such as ceramics and leather goods.

19 Morphett Street (corner with North Terrace), Adelaide
(08) 8410 0727 City Loop

Western Australia

Fremantle Arts Centre

An excellent Fremantle art gallery, which also sells a good selection of high-quality local arts and crafts.

1 Finnerty Street, Fremantle
(08) 9432 9555
Fremantle

Shopping Tours

Shopping is such big business in Australia (many visitors come with this activity very much in mind) that organised tours – usually concentrating on discounted factory and warehouse shopping – are common in the large cities. In Sydney you can join Shopping Spree ((02) 9360 6220), Melbourne offers the similarly named Shopping Spree Tours ((03) 9596 6600), while in South Australia, Adelaide Shopping Tours (1300 137 897) provide expert local knowledge.

Thrill Rides, Animal Parks & Fun Tours

Theme Parks
Children are exceptionally well catered for in Australia, with a wide range of museums, wildlife parks and other engrossing amusements. The theme parks are particularly good, including everything from the historical re-creations of Sovereign Hill in Victoria to the Gold Coast's educational Sea World and its entertainment complexes of Dreamworld, Wet 'n' Wild Water World and Warner Bros Movie World.

New South Wales

Featherdale Wildlife Park

This popular native wildlife park in Sydney's north-east contains some 2,000 animals. A great place to meet koalas, wombats, kangaroos, emus and many other bird species.

217 Kildare Road, Doonside, Sydney (02) 9622 1644 Daily 9–5 Blacktown then bus 725

Scenic World

With its Scenic Railway and Sceniscender rides deep into the valley, walking tracks, wildlife and forest boardwalk, Scenic World is ideal for families.

Corner Violet Street and Cliff Drive, Katoomba, Blue Mountains (02) 4782 2699 Daily 9–5 Katoomba

Sydney Olympic Park

Visit the 2000 Olympic Games site for its parklands, cafés and restaurants, a swim at the wonderful Sydney Aquatic Centre and tours of the Olympic stadium.

Homebush Bay, Sydney (02) 9714 7545 Daily (Visitor Centre 9–4:30, closed 25 Dec) Olympic Park Homebush Bay

Australian Capital Territory

Australian Institute of Sport

Sports-loving children will enjoy a tour of this national training centre and its excellent facilities. Tours are led by some of Australia's elite athletes.

Leverrier Crescent, Bruce (02) 6214 1444 (tours) Tours daily at 10, 11:30, 1 and 2. Closed 25 Dec 80

Queensland

Australian Woolshed

Just 20 minutes from Brisbane, you can watch sheep and sheepdog shows and visit the wildlife park.

148 Samford Road, Ferny Hills, Brisbane (07) 3872 1100 Daily 9–5 Ferny Grove

Lone Pine Koala Sanctuary

Close to Brisbane city, this sanctuary specialises in koalas but also contains kangaroos, wombats and other Australian animals.

Jesmond Road, Fig Tree Pocket, Brisbane (07) 3378 1366 Daily 8:30–5 River cruise from city centre

Tjapukai Aboriginal Cultural Park

North of Cairns, this exciting and educational complex includes dance shows, boomerang throwing, an Aboriginal camp and other aspects of indigenous culture.

Kamerunga Road, Smithfield, Cairns (07) 4042 9900 Daily 9–5 and some evenings Marlin Coast Sun Bus

Victoria

Healesville Sanctuary

There are over 200 species of Australian animals at this natural bushland sanctuary, just an hour from Melbourne.

Badger Creek Road, Healesville (03) 5957 2800 Daily 9–5 None

Scienceworks

A suburban Melbourne museum with fun, hands-on exhibits, live science shows and technological activities

2 Booker Street, Spotswood, Melbourne

(03) 9392 4800
Daily 10–4:30. Closed Good Fri, 25 Dec **Spotswood**

Tasmania

Bonorong Wildlife Park

An award-winning wildlife park near Hobart, where you can meet Tasmanian devils, wombats, koalas, kangaroos and other native Australian animals.

Briggs Road, Brighton
(03) 6268 1184 **Daily 9–5. Closed 25 Dec**
Tasmanian Redline bus from Hobart

Cadbury Chocolate Factory

Taking children on a tour of this tempting attraction near Hobart may be asking for trouble, but it's a fun experience! Bookings are essential and children must have adult supervision.

Cadbury Road, Claremont, Hobart **(03) 6249 0333**
Mon–Fri: tours from 8:30. Closed all public hols
Cruise or bus from Hobart

South Australia

Glenelg

Taking a tram to this seaside Adelaide suburb is great fun, and once there kids can enjoy the beach and the Magic Mountain fun fair.

Magic Mountain, Colley Reserve, Glenelg, Adelaide
(08) 8294 8199 **Mon–Fri 10–5, Sat–Sun 11–7** **Glenelg tram**

South Australian Maritime Museum

This fascinating museum will appeal to older children. There are moored vessels, interior exhibits and even a lighthouse.

126 Lipson Street, Port Adelaide **(08) 8207 6255**
Daily 10–5. Closed 25 Dec
Port Adelaide

Northern Territory

Aquascene

Every day at high tide, thousands of fish come here to be hand fed – an experience that should appeal to children.

28 Doctors Gully Road, Darwin **(08) 8981 7837**
Daily. Feeding times depend on tides **None**

Frontier Camel Farm

This operation offers both short and long rides from its camel farm. There is also a camel museum and a reptile house.

Ross River Highway, Alice Springs **(08) 8953 0444**
Daily 9–5 **None**

Western Australia

Rottnest Island

A day trip from Perth to this lovely island (➤ 89) is recommended. Children will enjoy the sandy beaches, clear waters and cute quokkas – small marsupials that roam the island.

Rottnest Island Visitor Centre, Thomson Bay
(08) 9372 9752 **Daily 8:30–5** **Rottnest Island**

AQWA

With its dolphin pool, sharks and examples of over 200 marine species, this aquarium in Perth's northern suburbs is a fun and educational destination for all the family.

Hillary's Boat Harbour, West Coast Highway, Sorrento
(08) 9447 7500
Daily 10–5. Closed 25 Dec
None

Outdoor Activities

Australia's Great Outdoors offers endless entertainment for youngsters. There are wonderful beaches to enjoy, national parks to explore, and outdoor activities such as horse riding. Most kids will also love the 'meet the sea creatures' events at Monkey Mia in Western Australia (dolphins), and in Darwin (hand feeding fish).

Theatre & Classical Entertainment

All Tastes Catered For
'Entertainment' in Australia covers everything from highbrow opera to high-spirited pubs and sporting activities of every kind. Most of the more cultural events are focused on the capital cities, but larger country towns, especially in New South Wales and Victoria, can offer surprisingly good theatre. Australians have a great love of gambling and there are casinos in each of the capital cities, as well as in Alice Springs, Launceston and on the Gold Coast.

New South Wales

Capitol Theatre

Sydney has many theatres, but this delightfully restored old building is the city's most charming. Major musicals are often performed here.

13 Campbell Street, Haymarket, Sydney
1300 855 445 **Central or Town Hall**

Sydney Opera House

It's not just opera that is performed here – the building includes venues for ballet, dance, classical music concerts and theatre.

Bennelong Point, Sydney
Box office (02) 6275 2700; administration (02) 6243 5711
Circular Quay

Australian Capital Territory

Canberra Theatre Centre

Canberra's main arts venue, for regular opera, ballet and theatre.

Civic Square, London Circuit, Canberra City
(02) 6275 2700 (tickets); (02) 6243 5711 (administration)
Any city-centre bus

Queensland

Queensland Performing Arts Centre

This large complex contains theatres and a concert hall, which host dance, theatre and orchestral events.

Queensland Cultural Centre, South Bank, Brisbane
(07) 3840 7444 or 13 6246
South Brisbane

Victoria

The Arts Centre

Melbourne's acclaimed arts centre hosts performances by the major Australian opera and dance companies and symphony orchestras.

100 St Kilda Road, Melbourne **(03) 9281 8000**
Tram 3, 5, 6, 8

Princess Theatre

This ornate 1887 city theatre is an atmospheric venue for plays and various other performances.

163 Spring Street, Melbourne **(03) 9299 9800**
City Circle tram

Tasmania

Theatre Royal

This charming 1830s theatre – Australia's oldest – is still used for plays and other performances.

29 Campbell Street, Hobart
(03) 6233 2299 **None**

South Australia

Adelaide Festival Centre

With its concert hall and theatres, this modern complex is Adelaide's premier performing arts venue.

King William Road, Adelaide **Administration (08) 8216 8600, tickets 13 1246**
City Loop

Northern Territory

Darwin Entertainment Centre

This large complex is the home of Darwin's concert, dance and theatre scene.

93 Mitchell Street, Darwin
(08) 8980 3333
None

Western Australia

His Majesty's Theatre

This charming early 1900s venue is the home of Perth theatre and opera.

825 Hay Street, Perth
(08) 9265 0900
Central Area Transit bus
Friends of the Theatre provide free theatre tours

Nightclubs & Casinos

New South Wales

Home

Sydney's largest and most popular nightclub, on the waterfront at Darling Harbour, with bars, dining, dancing and a great atmosphere.

Cockle Bay Wharf, Darling Harbour, Sydney (02) 9266 0600 Daily (Monorail) Darling Park

Star City

Sydney's vast casino complex near Darling Harbour operates 24 hours a day.

80 Pyrmont Street, Pyrmont, (02) 9777 9000 All day Light Rail

Australian Capital Territory

Casino Canberra

You don't have to be into gambling, as this small boutique-style casino has restaurants, bars and one of Canberra's liveliest nightclubs.

21 Binara Street, Canberra City (02) 6257 7074 Daily noon–6AM Any city-centre bus

Queensland

Conrad Jupiters Casino

The brash Gold Coast is the perfect venue for this glitzy casino complex, which offers a variety of entertainment.

Gold Coast Highway, Broadbeach, Gold Coast (07) 5592 8100 Daily 1, 1A

Friday's Riverside

With a great view of the river, this large Brisbane nightclub has everything. There are several restaurants, three bars, a few dance floors and live bands appearing regularly.

Riverside Centre, 123 Eagle Street, Brisbane (07) 3832 2122 Daily The Loop

Victoria

Melbourne Metro Nightclub

Here you will find progressive house and up-front dance music.

20–30 Bourke Street, Melbourne (03) 9663 4288 City Circle tram

Tasmania

Wrest Point Casino

Much more than a casino, Tasmania's premier nightspot offers dining, bars and live music.

410 Sandy Bay Road, Sandy Bay, Hobart (03) 6225 0112 Daily None

South Australia

SkyCity Adelaide Casino

This is worth visiting as much for the splendid architecture – a grand 1920s Adelaide railway station – as for its entertainment.

North Terrace, Adelaide (08) 8212 2811 Daily from 10AM. Closed Good Fri, 25 Dec City Loop

Northern Territory

MGM Grand Casino

This large beachfront casino complex is Darwin's most popular nightlife venue.

Gilruth Avenue, The Gardens, Darwin (08) 8943 8888 Daily None

Western Australia

Margeaux's

A classy nightclub in one of Perth's best hotels; it includes a bar and a disco.

Parmelia Hilton, 14 Mill Street, Perth (08) 9215 2000 Daily Central Area Transit bus

What's On

The best way to find out about the entertainment scene in each capital city is to study the local newspaper. The *Sydney Morning Herald*, for example, includes entertainment information every day, but this paper's Friday *Metro* guide is a comprehensive look at what's on during the coming week. The major newspapers also include information on where to obtain tickets for concerts and other events.

Pubs, Bars & Live Music

The Movies
The cinema is alive and well in Australia. You can see all the latest releases soon after they have opened in the northern hemisphere. Keep a look-out, too, for some of Australia's excellent home-grown movies – films like *Shine, Babe, Priscilla Queen of the Desert, Muriel's Wedding* and *Moulin Rouge* took the film world by storm. Check the various newspaper entertainment pages for full details of films and venues.

New South Wales

The Basement
An atmospheric club that specialises in live jazz, blues, funk and other music.
29 Reiby Place, Circular Quay, Sydney (02) 9251 2797 Daily Circular Quay

The Bridge Hotel
A lively Inner West pub, featuring live blues, jazz, soul, rock and other forms of music several nights a week.
135 Victoria Road, Rozelle (02) 9810 1260 Daily 500, 501, 502

Mercantile Hotel
One of Sydney's most character-filled pubs, with live Irish music and draught Guinness.
25 George Street, The Rocks, Sydney (02) 9247 3570 Daily Circular Quay

Australian Capital Territory

The Holy Grail
A popular bar and restaurant in trendy Kingston, offering live music from Wednesday to Saturday nights.
Green Square, Jardine Street, Kingston (02) 6295 6071 Daily 10–5 39, 83, 84

Queensland

Arena
This buzzing venue in Brisbane's main nightlife district features live bands, DJs and dancing on most nights of the week.
210 Brunswick Street, Fortitude Valley, Brisbane (07) 3252 5690 Daily 121, 204, 300

Press Club
The city's trendiest cafe and bar with a DJ playing cool music seven nights a week.
Cnr Brunswick and Ann Sreets, Fortitude Valley (07) 3852 4000 121, 204, 300

Victoria

The Purple Emerald
This groovy and retro-style bar plays live jazz five nights a week, Wednesday to Sunday.
191 Flinders Lane, Melbourne (03) 9650 7753 City Circle tram

Tasmania

Republic Bar & Café
In North Hobart's lively dining strip, the Republic offers Modern Australian cuisine and live music every night.
299 Elizabeth Street, North Hobart, Hobart (03) 6234 6954 Daily

South Australia

Cargo Club
A central Adelaide club; live jazz, soul and funk are a bonus on some nights.
213 Hindley Street West, Adelaide (08) 8231 2327 Live music Thu & Sun City Loop

Northern Territory

Shenannigans Irish Pub
A friendly Darwin pub, with bistro dining, a good range of beers and live entertainment.
69 Mitchell Street, Darwin (08) 8981 2100 Daily None

Western Australia

Metropolis City
This smart club is one of the Perth area's best venues for live music.
146 Roe Street, Northbridge, Perth (08) 9228 0500 Daily Central Area Transit bus

Sports & Adventures

Ballooning

Balloon Aloft
Hot-air ballooning is a great way to see Canberra's layout.
Canberra, Australian Capital Territory (02) 6285 1540 Daily at dawn from various locations None

Bushwalking

Tasmanian Expeditions
Tasmania's national parks and World Heritage Areas are wonderful for bushwalking. Novices are advised to join a guided tour.
23 Earl Street, Launceston, Tasmania (03) 6334 3477 None

Cricket and Australian Rules Football

Melbourne Cricket Ground
The famous Melbourne Cricket Ground is a must for sport fans – cricket is played here in summer, and Australian Rules football in winter.
Yarra Park, Jolimont, Melbourne, Victoria (03) 9657 8888 Trams 48, 75

Adelaide Oval
Watch exciting summer cricket matches, and winter Australian Rules football games.
King William Road, North Adelaide, South Australia (08) 8300 3800 182, 204, 222

Fishing

Darwin is an ideal departure point for game fishing, and many operators offer escorted trips – details are available from the local tourism association.
www.tourismtopend.com.au
Tourism Top End, Knuckey/Mitchell streets, Darwin, Northern Territory (08) 8936 2499 None

Golf

Palm Meadows
There are so many top golf courses around the Gold Coast that the area could be renamed the 'Golf Coast'. Palm Meadows is one of the best.
Palm Meadows Drive, Carrara, Gold Coast, Queensland (07) 5594 2450 Daily 1, 1A, 20

Burswood Resort Perth Golf Course
The Burswood is one of several fine golf courses around Perth.
Great Eastern Highway, Burswood, Perth, Western Australia (08) 9362 7777 Daily None

Skiing

Winter-sports fans who are visiting during the ski season should sample a ski field.
www.thredbo.com.au
Thredbo Village, New South Wales 1800 020 589, Mid-Jun to early Oct, daily Cooma, then a bus

Swimming

North Sydney Olympic Pool
A swim at this harbourside pool (open air in summer) is a great experience.
North Sydney Olympic Pool, Alfred Street, Milsons Point, Sydney (02) 9955 2309 Mon–Fri 5:30AM–9PM, Sat–Sun 7–7 Milsons Point

Outdoor Entertainment
Australia's climate lends itself to outdoor entertainment, and there are many alfresco events for visitors to enjoy. In Melbourne, regular events take place at the Myer Music Bowl; in Sydney, January brings open-air opera and classical music concerts in The Domain; while Darwin offers the outdoor Deckchair Cinema at Wharf Precinct most evenings from April to November. There are also free concerts in public spaces and parkland throughout the nation in the summer months.

What's On When

Gay and Lesbian Mardi Gras

Australia's most colourful and well-attended festival is Sydney's Gay and Lesbian Mardi Gras. The festival's spectacular street parade, staged in late February or early March, has grown from humble beginnings in 1978 to attract as many as 700,000 spectators and some 6,000 participants each year.

As a nation, Australia spends a considerable amount of time in holiday and party mode. There are nine annual national public holidays, and each state holds at least one major festival each year. These range from the highbrow cultural events of the Adelaide, Melbourne and Sydney festivals to sporting carnivals and the bizarre Henley-on-Todd Regatta at the waterless Alice Springs .

January
Mid- to late Jan – Australian Open (tennis, Melbourne).
26 – Australia Day holiday.
All month – Sydney Festival.

February
Variable – Chinese New Year Festival (around Australia).
All month – Sydney Gay and Lesbian Mardi Gras (➤ panel).
Feb/Mar – Adelaide Festival and Adelaide Fringe Festival (even-numbered years only).
Mid-Feb to early Mar – Perth International Arts Festival.

March
Mar to Apr – Melbourne International Comedy Festival
Early Mar – Australian Formula One Grand Prix (motor racing, Melbourne).
Early to mid-Mar – Canberra National Multicultural Festival.
Late Mar or early Apr – Barossa Vintage Festival (odd-numbered years only); Royal Easter Show (Sydney).

April
25 – Anzac Day holiday.

May
Early May – Bangtail Muster (parade, Alice Springs).

June
Wintersun Carnival (Gold Coast).

July
Mid-Jul – Lions Camel Cup Carnival (camel races, Alice Springs).
All month – Darwin Cup Carnival (horse racing).
Late July – Royal Darwin Show.

August
Early or mid-Aug – City to Surf fun run (Sydney).
Aug to Sep – Festival of Darwin.
Late Aug – Alice Springs Rodeo.

September
Early Sep to early Oct – Brisbane Festival (Performing Arts)
Late Sep – AFL Grand Final (Australian Rules football, Melbourne).
Mid-Sep to mid-Oct – Floriade Spring Festival (Canberra).
Henley-on-Todd Regatta (Alice Springs).
Reef Festival of Cairns.

October
Mid-Oct – Indy Carnival (motor racing, Gold Coast)
Manly International Jazz Festival (Sydney).
Melbourne International Arts Festival.

November
First Tue – Melbourne Cup horse race.
Late Nov – Fremantle Festival.

December
Late Dec to Jan – Hobart Summer Festival.

Practical Matters

Before You Go 118
When You Are There 119–23
Language 124

Above: *Captain Cook Cruises, Sydney*
Right: *totem pole at the Australian Museum, Sydney*

TIME DIFFERENCES

GMT	Australia (Sydney)	Germany	USA (NY)	Netherlands	Spain
12 noon	10PM	1PM	7AM	1PM	1PM

BEFORE YOU GO

WHAT YOU NEED

● Required
○ Suggested
▲ Not required

Some countries require a passport to remain valid for a minimum period (usually at least six months) beyond the date of entry – contact their consulate or embassy or your travel agent for details.

	UK	Germany	USA	Netherlands	Spain
Passport (valid for six months from date of entry)	●	●	●	●	●
Visa (or Electronic Travel Authority – ETA)	●	●	●	●	●
Onward or Return Ticket	●	●	●	●	●
Health Inoculations	▲	▲	▲	▲	▲
Health Documentation (reciprocal agreement document) (➤ 123, Health)	●	▲	▲	●	▲
Travel Insurance	●	●	●	●	●
Driving License (national) and International Driving Permit	●	●	●	●	●

WHEN TO GO

Australia (Sydney)

High season: JAN–APR, AUG–DEC
Low season: MAY–JUL

JAN	FEB	MAR	APR	MAY	JUN	JUL	AUG	SEP	OCT	NOV	DEC
26°C	26°C	25°C	22°C	19°C	17°C	16°C	18°C	20°C	22°C	24°C	25°C
Sun	Sun	Sunshine & showers	Wet	Wet	Sunshine & showers	Sunshine & showers	Sunshine & showers	Sunshine & showers	Sunshine & showers	Sun	Sun

Sun Sunshine & showers Wet

TOURIST OFFICES

In the UK
Australian Tourist Commission
Gemini House
10–18 Putney Hill
London SW15 6AA
☎ 020 8780 2229
Fax 020 8780 1496

In the USA
Australian Tourist Commission
2049 Century Park East
Suite 1920
Los Angeles CA 90067
☎ 310/229 4870
Fax 310/552 1215

Website
www.australia.com

POLICE 000

FIRE 000

AMBULANCE 000

OTHER SERVICES – See local phone book

WHEN YOU ARE THERE

ARRIVING

All major airlines operate services to Australia. Qantas, the Australian national airline, flies from London to Australia's international airports. Flights from Europe take between 20 and 30 hours; flights from North America take about 15 hours.

Sydney Airport
Kilometres to city centre

10 kilometres

Journey times
20 minutes
35 minutes
25 minutes

Darwin Airport
Kilometres to city centre

12.5 kilometres

Journey times
N/A
15 minutes
15 minutes

MONEY

The monetary unit of Australia is the Australian dollar ($A) and the cent (100 cents = 1 $A dollar).

Coins come in 5¢, 10¢, 20¢, 50¢ and $1 and $2 denominations, and there are $5, $10, $20, $50 and $100 notes.

Major credit cards are accepted in all large cities and most airports and banks have facilities for changing foreign currency and traveller's checks.

TIME

Australia has three time zones. Perth (WA) is 8 hours ahead of GMT (GMT+8) and Sydney (NSW) is 10 hours ahead of GMT (GMT+10). Daylight Saving Time varies from state to state.

CUSTOMS

YES

Airports have inbound duty-free stores. There are duty-free allowances for those over 18 years of age.
Alcohol: spirits: 1.125L
Cigarettes: 250 *or*
Tobacco: 250gm
Perfume or toilet water: no limit but a duty/tax free allowance of $A400 per person over 18 and $A200 per person under 18 is available for goods intended as gifts. These articles must accompany you through customs and must not be intended for commercial purposes. There are no restrictions on the import or export of Australian currency although a report form must be completed for amounts over $A10,000.
www.customs.gov.au

NO

Drugs, steroids, weapons, firearms, protected wildlife and associated products. There are very strict regulations governing the importation of foods, plants and animals.

CONSULATES

UK	Germany	USA	Netherlands	Spain
☎ (02) 6270 6666	☎ (02) 6270 1911	☎ (02) 6214 5600	☎ (02) 6273 3111	☎ (02) 6273 3555
Canberra	Canberra	Canberra	Canberra	Canberra

WHEN YOU ARE THERE

TOURIST OFFICES

- Canberra Visitor Centre (ACT)
  330 Northbourne Avenue
  Dickson 2602
  ☎ (02) 6205 0044

- Sydney Visitor Centre (NSW)
  106 George Street
  The Rocks
  ☎ (02) 9240 8788

- Queensland Travel Centre
  30 Makerston Street
  Brisbane 4000
  ☎ (07) 3535 4557

- Western Australia Visitor Centre, Forrest Place (cnr Wellington Street)
  Perth 6000
  ☎ (08) 9483 1111

- Tourism Top End (NT)
  Beagle House
  Knuckey/Mitchell streets
  Darwin 0800
  ☎ (08) 8936 2499

- South Australia Visitor & Travel Centre
  18 King William Street
  Adelaide 3000
  ☎ (08) 8303 2220

- Melbourne Visitor Information Centre
  Federation Square
  Melbourne 3000
  ☎ (03) 9658 9658

- Tasmanian Travel & Information Centre
  20 Davey Street
  Hobart 7000
  ☎ (03) 6230 8233

NATIONAL HOLIDAYS

J	F	M	A	M	J	J	A	S	O	N	D
2		(2)	(1/3)		1						2

1 Jan	New Year's Day
26 Jan	Australia Day
Variable	Labour Day
Mar/Apr	Good Friday
Mar/Apr	Easter Monday
25 Apr	Anzac Day
Jun (second Mon)	Queen's Birthday
25 Dec	Christmas Day
26 Dec	Boxing Day

In addition, individual states have public holidays throughout the year for agricultural shows, e.g. Brisbane Royal Show; regattas and race days, e.g. Melbourne Cup Day.

OPENING HOURS

○ Shops ● Post Offices
● Offices ● Museums/Monuments
● Banks ● Pharmacies

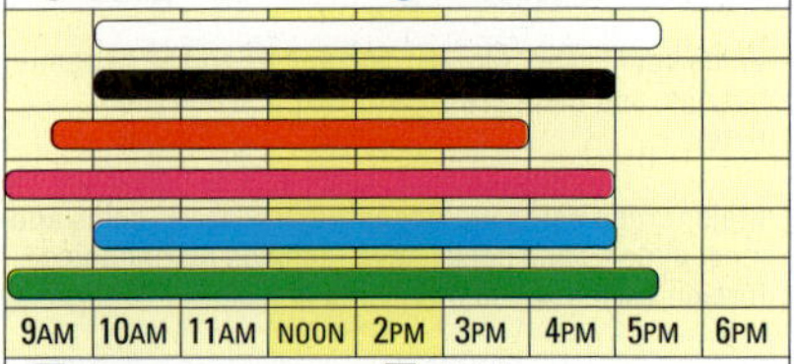

☐ Day ☐ Midday
☐ Evening

Shop opening hours vary from state to state. Many supermarkets and department stores have late night opening on Thursday or Friday until 8 or 9PM and are open 9AM–5PM on Saturday. Shops in tourist centres and pedestrianised areas in cities are often open on Sunday. Some pharmacies are open longer hours than shown above and offer a 24-hour service in big cities. Opening times of museums may vary.

DRIVE ON THE
LEFT

TOILETS
FREE

PUBLIC TRANSPORT

Internal Flights Australia has a wide network of domestic and regional air services. Many airlines offer outstanding discount deals, but check before departure whether you need to purchase tickets or passes before you go. Qantas and Virgin Blue are the main domestic airlines. Contact your travel agent for full details.

Trains Most capital cities have frequent services between business districts and the suburbs. Long-distance trains offer sleeping berths and reclining seats, and most interstate trains have dining or buffet cars. Reservations are accepted up to nine months in advance on long-distance trains. Leisure Rail ☎ (UK) 0870 7500 2222.

Bus travel Excellent long-distance express bus services run daily between major cities, serviced by McCafferty's Greyhound (☎ 132 030 or 131 499). Coaches are non-smoking, have air-conditioning and bathrooms. Tasmania is serviced by Tasmanian Redline Coaches and Tassie Link.

Ferries The only regular interstate ferry services are the overnight *Spirit of Tasmania* passenger/vehicle ferries between Melbourne and Devonport in Tasmania (daily service) and Sydney and Devonport (twice weekly in winter, three times weekly at other times). ☎ 1800 634 906; www.spiritoftasmania.com.au

Urban Transport Most state capital cities have good train services and/or frequent bus services that operate between the city centre and the suburbs. Perth, Brisbane and Sydney also have regular local ferry services, and trams or light railways run in Melbourne, Adelaide and Sydney. Smoking is not permitted in any public vehicles.

CAR RENTAL

Rental cars/motorhomes are available at major air and rail terminals and from cities throughout Australia. It is advisable to book, especially during December and January. Most rental companies offer advice and provide relevant guides and maps.

TAXIS

Except in some country towns, all taxis in Australia operate on a meter system. All fares are as displayed on the meter. Taxis can be booked (at an extra charge) or they can be stopped on the street. Smoking is not permitted in any public vehicles.

DRIVING

Speed limit on motorways: **100–110kph**

Speed limit on all country roads: **100kph**

Speed limit on urban roads: **40–60kph**

It is compulsory for drivers and passengers to wear seat belts at all times.

Random breath-testing. Never drive under the influence of alcohol.

Fuel comes in leaded and unleaded grades and is sold by the litre. Filling stations are plentiful, except in some Outback areas, but trading hours vary. Most service stations accept international credit cards.

If your hire car breaks down you should contact the rental company, which will arrange to send road service to your location and repair the vehicle. Alternatively, most service stations will be able to assist or, at least, direct you to the nearest repair centre. Check with your own motoring club regarding reciprocal facilities.

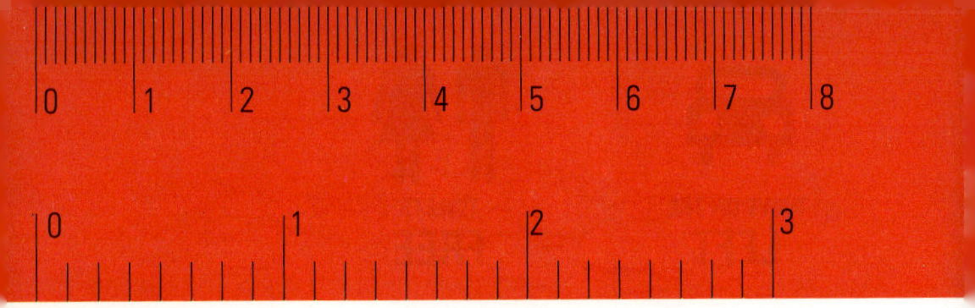

PERSONAL SAFETY

In crowded places, the usual safety precautions should be taken. Walking in the bush and swimming have their hazards.

- Hitch-hiking is not recommended: this is illegal in some states.
- Women should avoid walking alone at night.
- If bushwalking or camping, leave an itinerary with friends. Wear boots, socks and trousers.
- Take care and heed warning signs when swimming, whether in the sea or fresh water (crocodiles!)

Police assistance:
☎ **000**
from any phone

TELEPHONES

Long-distance calls within Australia (STD) and International Direct Dialling (IDD) can be made on public payphones (check with operator for charges). Public payphones accept cash and *Phonecard*, which is available from retail outlets in denominations of $A5, $A10 and $A20. The *International Direct* service gives access to over 50 countries for collect or credit card calls. Phones that accept credit cards can be found at airports, central city locations and many hotels. A *Telstra PhoneAway* prepaid card enables you to use virtually any phone in Australia with all call costs charged against the card.

International Dialling Codes

From Australia to:	
UK:	**0011 44**
Germany:	**0011 49**
USA/Canada:	**0011 1**
Netherlands:	**0011 31**
Spain:	**0011 34**

POST

Post Offices
The offices of Australia Post are located in city centres and suburbs and are often combined with a general store in smaller places. Postal and *poste restante* services are available. Open Mon–Fri 9–5 . Mail boxes are painted red with a white stripe.

ELECTRICITY

The power supply is: 220/240 volts, 50 cycles AC. Sockets accept three-flat-pin plugs so you may need an adaptor. If your appliances are 110v check if there is a 110/240v switch; if not you will need a voltage converter. Universal outlets for 240v or 110v shavers are usually found in leading hotels.

TIPS/GRATUITIES

Yes ✓ No ✕		
Restaurants (service not incl)	✓	10%
Bar service	✕	
Taxis	✕	
Tour guides		optional
Hairdressers	✕	
Chambermaids	✕	
Porters (hotel) per bag	✓	$A1–2
Theatre/cinema attendants	✕	
Cloakroom attendants	✕	
Toilets	✕	

PHOTOGRAPHY

What to photograph: The wilderness, Barrier Reef, mountains, lakes, rivers, dramatic coastal scenery, modern architecture.
When to photograph: In the Outback allow for exceptional intensity of light; best to photograph early in the morning or late afternoon. Allow for reflected light at coastal locations.
Where to buy film: There are plenty of camera shops in all big cities; excellent developing and printing services are available.

HEALTH

Insurance

British and certain other nationals are eligible for free basic care at public hospitals but it is strongly recommended that all travellers take out a comprehensive medical insurance policy.

Dental Services

Dentists are plentiful and the standard of treatment is high – as are the bills. In an emergency go to the casualty wing of a local hospital, or locate a dentist from the local telephone book. Medical insurance is essential.

Sun Advice

The sun in Australia is extremely strong, especially in summer. Wear a hat to protect your face and neck, and sunglasses to protect your eyes. Avoid sunbathing in the middle of the day. Use a high-factor sunscreen and wear long sleeves.

Drugs

Prescription and non-prescription drugs are available from chemists or pharmacies. Visitors may import up to three months' supply of prescribed medication: bring a doctor's certificate.

Safe Water

It is safe to drink tap water throughout Australia. Bottled mineral water is available throughout the country.

CONCESSIONS

Students/Youths Young visitors should join the International Youth Hostels Federation before leaving their own country. Australia has a widespread network of youth and backpacker hostels. International Student or Youth Identity Cards may entitle the holder to discounts on attractions.

Senior Citizens Many attractions offer a discount for senior citizens; the age limit varies from 60 to 65, and your passport should be sufficient evidence of age. However, few discounts on travel are available to overseas senior citizens, as an Australian pension card is usually required to qualify.

CLOTHING SIZES

Australia	UK	Europe		
36	36	46	36	Suits
38	38	48	38	
40	40	50	40	
42	42	52	42	
44	44	54	44	
46	46	56	46	
7	7	41	8	Shoes
7½	7½	42	8½	
8½	8½	43	9½	
9½	9½	44	10½	
10½	10½	45	11½	
11	11	46	12	
14½	14½	37	14½	Shirts
15	15	38	15	
15½	15½	39/40	15½	
16	16	41	16	
16½	16½	42	16½	
17	17	43	17	
8	8	34	6	Dresses
10	10	36	8	
12	12	38	10	
14	14	40	12	
16	16	42	14	
18	18	44	16	
4½	4½	37½	6	Shoes
5	5	38	6½	
5½	5½	38½	7	
6	6	39	7½	
6½	6½	40	8	
7	7	41	8½	

WHEN DEPARTING

- The airport departure tax when leaving Australia is incorporated into the price of your air ticket.
- Contact the airline at least 72 hours before departure to 'reconfirm' your seat.
- Arrive at the airport at least 2 hours before your departure time to avoid getting 'bumped' and to allow for security checks and immigration procedures.

LANGUAGE

The common language of Australia is English, but it has been adapted and modified to form 'Strine', a colourful and abbreviated version of the mother tongue. The rather nasal Australian accent is quite distinctive and is spoken without any real regional variation throughout the country. The vocabulary contains a number of words of Aboriginal origin (didgeridoo and kangaroo), but the real joy of 'Strine' is its slang. The following is a short list of words and abbreviations you may encounter.

Australian	**English**
ABC	Australian Broadcasting Corporation
ACT	Australian Capital Territory (Canberra Area)
ALP	Australian Labor Party
ANZAC	Australian and New Zealand Army Corps
arvo	afternoon
barbie	barbecue
bludger	scrounger
blue	a fight, or a redhead
bottle shop	off license/liquor store
bush	countryside
BYO	bring your own (drink to a restaurant)
cask	wine-box
chook	chicken
chunder	to vomit
cockie	farmer
crook	ill
drongo	slow-witted person
dunny	outside lavatory
esky	large insulated box for keeping beer or refreshments cold
fossicking	hunting for precious stones
galah	a kind of parrot, an idiot
garbo	garbage collector
g'day	good day, traditional Australian greeting
interstate	anything to do with the other Australian states
jackaroo	young male trainee on a station (farm)
joey	baby kangaroo
lair, larrikin	rogue, layabout, ruffian
lamington	a square of sponge cake covered in chocolate icing and coconut
lollies	sweets, candy
ocker	an Australian male with crude manners
ripper	good (also 'little ripper')
sandshoes	trainers, sneakers
semi-trailer	articulated truck
shoot through	to leave
snags	sausages
sprog	baby
station	large farm or ranch
strides	trousers
stubby	small bottle of beer
Tassie	Tasmania
tinny	can of beer
uni	university
unit	apartment, flat
ute	utility truck (pickup truck)
wowser	prude, killjoy
yakka	work

INDEX

Aboriginal culture 13, 21, 22, 26, 34, 36, 43, 49, 52, 59, 63, 66, 73, 77, 79, 80, 85, 89, 104–5, 124
accommodation 100–103
Adelaide 72–73, 76
Adelaide Botanic Garden 76
Adelaide Hills 77
Adelaide Zoo 76
Albany 88
Alice Springs 80
Anglesea 20
Antartic Adventure 66
animal parks 110, 111
Armadale 90
Arnhem Land 21
Art Gallery of New South Wales 36
Art Gallery of South Australia 73
Atherton Tableland 16
Australian Aviation Heritage Centre 81
Australian Capital Territory (ACT) 30, 42–43
Australian Institute of Sport 110
Australian Museum 34
Australian National Botanic Gardens 42
Australian Stockman's Hall of Fame 53
Australian War Memorial 43
Ayers Rock *see* Uluru-Kata Tjuta National Park

Ballarat 63
banks 120
Barossa Valley 77
Batchelor 81
Bathurst Island 69
Battery Point 66
Berrima 40
Berry Springs 81
Bicheno 66
Blackall Range 54
Blackheath 41
Blue Mountains 23, 41
Brisbane 48–49
Brisbane Botanic Gardens 49
Broken Hill 37
Broome 22
Bunbury 90
Bungle Bungles 22
buses 121
Byron Bay 37

Cairns 16, 55
Canberra 30, 42–43
Carnarvon National Park 52
car rental 121
Charters Towers 52
children's attractions 110–11
City Botanic Gardens, Brisbane 49
climate 118, 123
clothing sizes 123
Coffs Harbour 37
concessions 123
Coober Pedy 69
Coolgardie 88
Cooloola National Park 54
Coonawarra region 77
Cradle Mountain-Lake St Clair National Park 25
customs regulations 107, 119

Daintree National Park 55
Dandenong Ranges 63
Darling Harbour 34
Darwin 79, 81
Darwin Crocodile Farm 81
departure information 124
Devil's Marbles Conservation Reserve 80
Dorrigo National Park 37
drives
  Blue Mountains 41
  Cairns to the Daintree 55
  Darwin to Litchfield National Park 81
  South of Perth 90
driving 118, 121

eating out 68, 92–99
electricity 122
embassies and consulates 120
emergency telephone numbers 119, 122
entertainment 112–16

fauna and flora 12–13
festivals and events 116
Flagstaff Hill Maritime Museum 20
Flinders Ranges 77
food and drink 44–45
Franklin-Gordon Wild Rivers National Park 25, 67
Fraser Island 53
Fremantle 85
Freycinet Peninsula 66

Geikie Gorge National Park 22
geography 7
George Brown Darwin Botanic Gardens 79
Glenelg 73
Gold Coast 17
Great Barrier Reef 7, 9, 18–19, 47
Great Ocean Road 20

Hartz Mountains National Park 25
health 118, 123
history 10–11
Hobart 65–66
Hunter Valley 38

Jervis Bay 69

Kakadu National Park 13, 21
Kalgoorlie-Boulder 88
Kangaroo Island 77
Katherine 80
Kiama 39
the Kimberley 22
Kings Domain 62
Kings Park 85
Koala Conservation Centre 63
Kosciuszko National Park 40

Lamington National Park 17, 53
language 124
Launceston 66
Leura 41
Litchfield National Park 81
Longreach 53
Lord Howe Island 40
Lorne 20

MacDonnell Ranges 80
Macquarie Street, Sydney 36
Magnetic Island 54
Mandurah 90
maps
  Australia 28–29
  New South Wales 38–39
  Northern Territory 78
  Queensland 50–51
  South Australia 74–75
  Sydney 32–33
  Tasmania 64–65
  Victoria 60–61
  Western Australia 86–87
Margaret River 88–89
Marlin Coast 55
Melbourne 58–62
Melbourne Cricket Ground 59
Melbourne Observation Deck 59
Melbourne Museum 59
Melville Island 69
the Midlands 67
Mindil Beach 79
Minnamurra Rainforest Centre 39
money 119
Mossman Gorge 55
Mount Coot-tha 49
Mount Tamborine 17
Mount Tomah Botanic Garden 41
Mount Victoria 41
museums 120
Museum and Art Gallery of the Northern Territory 79
Myall Lakes National Park 40

Nambung National Park 89
Narryna Heritage Museum 66
National Gallery of Australia 43
National Gallery of Victoria 59
National Maritime Museum 34
National Motor Museum 77
National Museum of Australia 43
national holidays 120
national parks and reserves 12
New South Wales 23, 30–43
Ningaloo Reef 69
Nitmiluk National Park 80
Noosa Heads 54
Norfolk Island 69

Norman Lindsay Gallery and Museum 41
Northern Territory 21, 26, 71, 78–81,111

Oatlands 67
Old Melbourne Gaol 59
Old Telegraph Station 80
opening hours 120
Otway National Park 20

Parliament House 43
passports and visas 118
Pemberton 89
personal safety 122
Perth 84–85
pharmacies 120
Phillip Island 63
the Pinnacles 89
police 122
population 7
Port Arthur 67
Port Campbell 20
Port Campbell National Park 20
Port Douglas 55
Port Fairy 20
postal services 120, 122
Powerhouse Museum 34
public transport 121

Queensland 16–19, 46–55
Queensland Cultural Centre 49
Queensland Maritime Museum 49
Queensland Sciencentre 49
Questacon 43

Rockingham 90
The Rocks 35
Ross 67
Rottnest Island 89, 111
Royal Botanic Gardens, Melbourne 62
Royal Botanic Gardens, Sydney 36
Royal Flying Doctor Service 22, 37, 80, 88
Royal Tasmanian Botanical Gardens 66

St George's Terrace 85
St Kilda 60
Salamanca Place 66
Scienceworks 110–11
Seal Bay Conservation Park 77
Shark Bay 89
Shipwreck Coast 20
shopping 104–109, 120
Snowy Mountains 40
South Australia 71, 72–77, 111
South Australian Maritime Museum 111
South Australian Museum 73
Southern Highlands 40
Southwest National Park 25
Sovereign Hill 63
sport and leisure 69, 115
states and territories 7
Stirling Range National Park 88
Strahan 67
Sunshine Coast 54
Surfers Paradise 17
Sydney 24, 31–36
Sydney Harbour 9, 24
Sydney Harbour Bridge 24, 35
Sydney Opera House 9, 24, 36
Sydney Tower 35

Tandanya National Aboriginal Cultural Institute 73
Taronga Zoo 35
Tasman Peninsula 67
Tasmania 25, 57, 64–67, 111
Tasmanian Devil Park 67
Tasmanian Museum and Art Gallery 66
Tasmanian Wool Centre 67
taxis 121
telephones 122
theme parks 110
time 118, 119
tipping 122
Tjapukai Aboriginal Cultural Park 110
toilets 121
tourist offices 118, 120
Townsville 54
trains 121
travelling to Australia 119
Tuart Forest National Park 90

Uluṟu-Kata Tjuṯa National Park 9, 26

Victoria 20, 57, 58–63

walks
  Adelaide 76
  Melbourne 62
  Sydney 36
Warrawong Earth Sanctuary 77
Watarrka National Park 80
Wave Rock 89
Wentworth Falls 41
Western Australia 22, 82–90, 111
Western Australian Botanic Garden 85
Western Australian Maritime Museum 85
Western Australian Museum 85
Whitsunday Islands 54
William Ricketts Sanctuary 63
Wilpena Pound 77
Wilsons Promontory National Park 63
wine, beer, spirits 38, 45, 77, 88
Wolfe Creek Crater 22
World Heritage areas 12, 25

Yalgorup National Park 90

Acknowledgments
The Automobile Association would like to thank the following photographers, libraries and associations for their assistance in the preparation of this book.

AUSTRALIA POST 122r; AUSTRALIAN TOURIST COMMISSION 11c, 14c, 15b, 18/19, 19, 23, 27t, 28, 29, 36, 64t, 67, 73b, 76c, 79; BRUCE COLEMAN COLLECTION 6c, 22, 25c, 81c; INTERNATIONAL PHOTOBANK 15t, 16t, 16b, 17t, 18t, 20t, 21t, 22t, 23t, 23c, 24t, 25t, 26t; MARY EVANS PICTURE LIBRARY 10c; MRI BANKERS GUIDE TO FOREIGN CURRENCY 119; PICTURES COLOUR LIBRARY 53, 88/89; REX FEATURES LTD 14; SPECTRUM COLOUR LIBRARY 17b, 21c, 47, 50t, 50c, 52, 55t, 55c, 72, 122l; STOCK MARKET PHOTO AGENCY INC. 54; TOURISM VICTORIA 61

The remaining photographs are held in the Association's own library (AA WORLD TRAVEL LIBRARY) and were taken by ADRIAN BAKER with the exception of:
BILL BACHMAN 20c, 59; PETER BAKER 7c; PAUL KENWARD 1, 2, 5t, 6t, 6b, 7t, 8t, 9t, 9c, 9b, 10t, 12t, 14t, 24b, 27b, 30, 31t, 32, 33, 35, 40, 41t, 41c, 43, 44t, 44c, 45t, 45b, 91b, 117t, 117b; CHRISTINE OSBOURNE 56, 57, 58tl, 58tr, 61, 62t, 63, 68t, 69t, 75b

Abbreviations for the above – (t) top; (b) bottom; (c) centre; (l) left; (r) right

Contributors
Revision Management: Pam Stagg
Indexer: Marie Lorimer **Page Layout**: Design 23

Dear Essential Traveller

Your comments, opinions and recommendations are very important to us. So please help us to improve our travel guides by taking a few minutes to complete this simple questionnaire.

You do not need a stamp (unless posted outside the UK). If you do not want to cut this page from your guide, then photocopy it or write your answers on a plain sheet of paper.

Send to: **The Editor, AA World Travel Guides, FREEPOST SCE 4598, Basingstoke RG21 4GY.**

Your recommendations...

We always encourage readers' recommendations for restaurants, nightlife or shopping – if your recommendation is used in the next edition of the guide, we will send you a ***FREE*** **AA *Essential* Guide** of your choice. Please state below the establishment name, location and your reasons for recommending it.

____

____

____

____

Please send me **AA *Essential*** ____________________

About this guide...

Which title did you buy?
AA *Essential* ________________________

Where did you buy it? ________________________

When? m m / y y

Why did you choose an AA *Essential* Guide? ________________

____

____

____

____

Did this guide meet your expectations?
Exceeded ☐ Met all ☐ Met most ☐ Fell below ☐
Please give your reasons ________________________

____

____

____

continued on next page...

Were there any aspects of this guide that you particularly liked? ________

____

____

Is there anything we could have done better? ________________

____

____

About you...

Name (*Mr/Mrs/Ms*) ______________________________

Address ______________________________________

____

______________________ Postcode ________________

Daytime tel nos ______________________________

Please only give us your mobile phone number if you wish to hear from us about other products and services from the AA and partners by text or mms.

Which age group are you in?

Under 25 ☐ 25–34 ☐ 35–44 ☐ 45–54 ☐ 55–64 ☐ 65+ ☐

How many trips do you make a year?

Less than one ☐ One ☐ Two ☐ Three or more ☐

Are you an AA member? Yes ☐ No ☐

About your trip...

When did you book? m m / y y When did you travel? m m / y y

How long did you stay? ______________________________

Was it for business or leisure? ________________________

Did you buy any other travel guides for your trip?

If yes, which ones? ______________________________

Thank you for taking the time to complete this questionnaire. Please send it to us as soon as possible, and remember, you do not need a stamp (*unless posted outside the UK*).

Happy Holidays!

The information we hold about you will be used to provide the products and services requested and for identification, account administration, analysis, and fraud/loss prevention purposes. More details about how that information is used is in our privacy statement, which you'll find under the heading "Personal Information" in our terms and conditions and on our website: www.theAA.com. Copies are also available from us by post, by contacting the Data Protection Manager at AA, Southwood East, Apollo Rise, Farnborough, Hampshire GU14 OJW.

We may want to contact you about other products and services provided by us, or our partners (by mail, telephone) but please tick the box if you DO NOT wish to hear about such products and services from us by mail or telephone. ☐